Backpackers' Sourcebook

A Book of Lists

Penny Hargrove and Noëlle Liebrenz

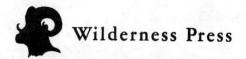

Wilderness Press

First edition 1979
SECOND EDITION 1983

Copyright © 1979, 1983 by Wilderness Press. All rights reserved.
Library of Congress Card Catalog Number 82-50739
International Standard Book Number 0-89997-025-7

Cover by Larry Van Dyke

Published by Wilderness Press
2440 Bancroft Way
Berkeley CA 94704

Write for free catalog.

Table of Contents

Checklist

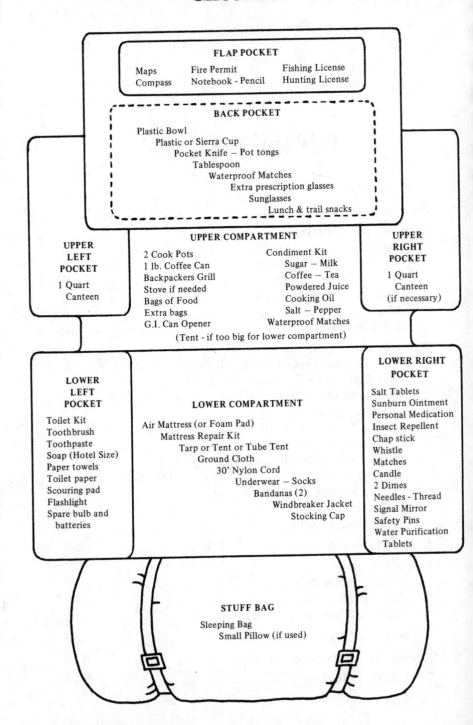

FLAP POCKET

Maps   Fire Permit   Fishing License
Compass   Notebook - Pencil   Hunting License

BACK POCKET

Plastic Bowl
Plastic or Sierra Cup
Pocket Knife — Pot tongs
Tablespoon
Waterproof Matches
Extra prescription glasses
Sunglasses
Lunch & trail snacks

UPPER LEFT POCKET

1 Quart Canteen

UPPER COMPARTMENT

2 Cook Pots   Condiment Kit
1 lb. Coffee Can   Sugar — Milk
Backpackers Grill   Coffee — Tea
Stove if needed   Powdered Juice
Bags of Food   Cooking Oil
Extra bags   Salt — Pepper
G.I. Can Opener   Waterproof Matches
(Tent - if too big for lower compartment)

UPPER RIGHT POCKET

1 Quart Canteen (if necessary)

LOWER LEFT POCKET

Toilet Kit
Toothbrush
Toothpaste
Soap (Hotel Size)
Paper towels
Toilet paper
Scouring pad
Flashlight
Spare bulb and
  batteries

LOWER COMPARTMENT

Air Mattress (or Foam Pad)
Mattress Repair Kit
Tarp or Tent or Tube Tent
Ground Cloth
30' Nylon Cord
Underwear — Socks
Bandanas (2)
Windbreaker Jacket
Stocking Cap

LOWER RIGHT POCKET

Salt Tablets
Sunburn Ointment
Personal Medication
Insect Repellent
Chap stick
Whistle
Matches
Candle
2 Dimes
Needles - Thread
Signal Mirror
Safety Pins
Water Purification
  Tablets

STUFF BAG

Sleeping Bag
Small Pillow (if used)

Introduction

When we decided to put together a sourcebook for backpackers, we had two main ideas. The first was that there ought to be an *easy* way for backpackers to discover What's Out There in parks and forests and wilderness areas—where the trails are, how to locate trail guides and maps, where to write for permits, what to bring along—in short, all the sort of nitty-gritty, pre-trip busywork that can slow down the most organized backpacker. Our second idea was that, in compiling all this necessary information for backpackers, there ought to be a way we could make it available to them *inexpensively*. Hence the **Backpackers' Sourcebook**, a straightforward, no-frills Book of Lists for backpackers everywhere who only want a little help in getting a trip planned.

The **Sourcebook** is divided into 9 regions—New England, Mid-Atlantic, Southeast, Midwest, Southwest, Mountain, Pacific Northwest, California, and Alaska and Hawaii. Each section lists the area's National Parks, national forests and wilderness areas, with descriptions of respective sizes, facilities, regulations and features. Trail guides and maps of the different areas are listed, with information on where to get them.

Some backpackers need to order equipment and food through the mail, so the names and addresses of each region's largest mail-order equipment outlets are given. A handy equipment checklist will reassure the backpacker that he or she hasn't forgotten anything.

Most backpackers seem to thrive on a steady diet of printed matter about the subject, so we have listed trail guides to wild areas throughout the US and the names and addresses of their publishers. We also tell you about three regional backpacking newsletters and give you a Recommended Reading list of How To Do It and First Aid books.

Backpackers can find hiking companions and kindred spirits in the dozens of hiking clubs and outdoor organizations we have listed; and for those who yearn to hike a particularly long or famous trail, we have an inspiring list of Long and Famous Trails, with information on how to find out more about them, from the Appalachian Trail in the East to the Pacific Crest Trail in the West (with quite a few in between).

APPLICATION FOR WILDERNESS PERMIT
(Please supply all information requested.)

I plan to visit _____ Wilderness
                              (name)

Planned   Planned
starting date _____   finish date _____
              mo.   day   year   mo.   day   year

Location of entry _____
                              (name or description)

Location of exit _____
                              (name or description)

Primary method of travel _____
                              (foot, horse, ski, boat, etc.)

Number of people in group _____

Number of pack and saddle stock _____

Day trips only. Destination _____
                              (name or description)

Planned overnight camp locations   Approximate nights in camp
     (Give best estimate)

1. _____   _____

2. _____   _____

3. _____   _____

4. _____   _____

5. _____   _____

6. _____   _____

Organization/Group name _____
                                   (if applicable)

Name _____

Address _____

City _____ State _____ Zip _____

I agree to abide by all laws, rules, and regulations which apply to
this area. I will do my best to see that everyone in my group does
likewise.

_____   _____
  (Date)   (Applicant's signature)

Preparing For Your Trip

Permits

Permits make good sense for everyone, and you will find that you need one for many wilderness areas you plan to backpack in. Permits are useful for governing agencies (National Park Service, US Forest Service, etc.) because permits can tell them which areas are most heavily trafficked and need the strongest controls. (In some fragile or overused areas, quota systems are necessary.) The permit system also gives you a reason to check in with the local rangers and get useful information about trails, weather conditions and much more.

You can obtain a Wilderness Permit at ranger stations and Forest Service field offices near your point of entry (you can contact the Park or Forest headquarters to find out where the field offices are). In popular areas and during peak season, it is a good idea to obtain your permit by mail, in advance, by writing the park or forest headquarters. In our "Where To Go" section we list these agencies and their addresses.

A permit is always issued for a single trip during a specified period of time. Only one permit is required for a group traveling together. In general, if you are traveling through several parks and/or forests, you need get only one permit at your point of entry.

Most of the time, a Wilderness Permit also serves as a campfire permit, but in areas where fire danger is high, a special fire permit may be necessary.

If you want to save time and are planning to backpack in a wilderness area in California, Arizona or Nevada, a valuable 128-page booklet called *Wilderness Digest* can help you. *Wilderness Digest* gives *complete* information on permit procedures, maps, guidebooks, and rules for the separate wilderness areas. You can order by sending $4.50 to Wilderness Digest, Box 989, Lone Pine, CA 93545

Rules and Regulations

Although you will find that different rules and regulations apply to different types of wilderness (and we will list some of the rules you can expect to find), there are certain common-sense guidelines that apply to *any* wilderness experience. Here are some of them:

1. Plan your trip carefully. Know what to expect in terms of terrain, wildlife and climate. Take a detailed map with you.
2. Let other people know where you're going and when you expect to return. Leave word with friends, and once you're there, sign all trail registers. The registers will help others find you if you become lost.
3. Never travel alone, but if you must, then stick to frequently used trails in case you become sick or injured.
4. Bring suitable equipment, but don't load yourself down with more than you need. A lightweight ground cloth, sunburn lotion and insect repellent can make the difference between comfort and discomfort, but leave canned and bottled foods and your heavy frying pan at home.
5. Know how to take care of yourself in bad weather. In dense fog or in a storm, stop at once and make camp in a sheltered place. During lightning storms, stay off ridges, away from open meadows and away from isolated trees. If possible, find shelter among dense, small trees in a low area.
6. Know the signs of hypothermia. It can be a "silent killer."
7. If you think you are lost, take it easy and keep calm. Sit down and figure out where you are. Use your head, not your legs.
8. Three of anything (shouts, smokes, fires) are a sign of distress. If they are seen or heard, help will soon be on the way. Use these "three" signals only in emergencies.

These above guidelines will help you have a safe and comfortable trip. There are also several ways in which you can minimize the effect that *you* have on the wilderness you're traveling in:

1. Use a portable stove whenever possible, even if wood fires are legal.

2. Don't destroy growing trees and shrubs. Use no boughs for bed or shelter.
3. If you are backpacking in a group, limit its size. Large groups can be particularly destructive in the wilderness.
4. Don't bring a pet, even if there is no rule against it. Dogs are a disruptive element in any wilderness area.
5. Know how to build a small, safe fire.
6. Do not bury trash. Pack out what you bring in.
7. Select a toilet spot well away from streams, lakes, camp areas and trails.

In addition to these general guidelines there are some very specific regulations set forth by the National Park Service, the US Forest Service and other agencies for the use of different types of wilderness. These are the regulations that you can expect to find:

National Parks and Monuments

Hunting or trapping in the backcountry is prohibited. Fishing is allowed under state law (i.e., you may need a state license). Dogs and cats are not permitted in the backcountry of any Park—not even on a leash. Fires are permitted only in designated camping and picnic sites. A permit is often required for backcountry use.

Half of the National Parks charge no entrance fee. The other half charge $1-$3 per car. You can purchase a Golden Eagle Passport for $10, which for the calendar year will give you free entry to all the National Parks. There is usually a per-night camping fee at developed campgrounds in the Parks.

National Forests

Hunting and fishing are permitted with license in the proper season. A backcountry permit may or may not be required (it will also serve as your campfire permit). There is no main entrance to a national forest, so there is no entrance fee. A developed campground may have a camping fee, but backcountry use is free.

Wilderness and Primitive Areas

All the rules of national forests apply. In addition, no motorized vehicles are permitted.

"He who travels alone arrives alone."
Lawrence Ferlinghetti

6

Mail-Order Equipment

Proper equipment is essential for enjoyable backpacking. Your most important items of equipment will be good, comfortable footwear, your pack and your sleeping bag. Shop carefully for the equipment you buy: the proper gear, though sometimes expensive, can last a long time.

It is always best to *see* what you're buying before you purchase it, but if there are no backpacking equipment stores in your area, you can shop by mail from any of the stores we have listed here.

Adventure 16
4620 Alvarado Canyon Rd.
San Diego CA 92120

Camp Trails
Box 966
Binghamton NY 13902

Cannondale
35 Pulaski St.
Stamford CT 96902

Early Winters
110 Prefontaine Place So.
Seattle WA 98104

Eastern Mountain Sports
Vose Farm Road
Peterborough NH 03458

Eddie Bauer
Box 3700
Seattle WA 98124

JanSport
Paine Field Industrial Park
Everett WA 98204

L. L. Bean
Freeport ME 04032

Marmot Mountain Works
3040 Adeline
Berkeley CA 94703

Moonstone Mountaineering
Box 4206
Arcata CA 95521

Nippenose
330 Government Place
Williamsport PA 17701

The North Face
1234 Fifth St.
Berkeley CA 94710

Recreational Equipment
18200 Segale Park Dr. "B"
Tukwila WA 98188

Stephenson Warm-lite
RFD 4, Box 145
Gilford NH 03246

The Yak Works
2030 Westlake Ave.
Seattle WA 98121

There are also two ways in which you can beat the high cost of backpacking equipment. One way is to buy used equipment: sporting-goods stores often have bulletin boards, where individuals can sell directly to other individuals. Someone else's mistake, like the wrong-sized hiking boot, can mean a bargain for you. The other way is to make your own sleeping bag, parka, pack or whatever from a kit. Most kits have pre-cut pieces and excellent instructions. The following companies sell kits:

Frostline Kits
Frostline Circle
Denver CO 80241

Holubar Kits
Box 7
Boulder CO 80306

Country Ways
3500 Hwy 101 South
Minnetonka MN 55343

Mail-Order Foods

If you choose to go the "convenience" route in preparing meals while backpacking, you will find that most backpacking equipment stores sell freeze-dried foods (and also offer a selection through their mail-order catalog). However, if you prefer a larger selection, you can order direct from these companies:

Trail Foods Co.
Box 9309
No. Hollywood CA 91609

Stow-A-Way
166 Cushing Hwy
Cohasset MA 02025

In addition, we list these two companies, probably the largest whole-salers of freeze-dried foods. They will not sell directly to you, but they will, if you write them, supply you with a list of dealers in your area.

Oregon Freeze Dry Foods, Inc.
Box 1048
Albany OR 97321

Rich-Moor
Box 2728
Van Nuys CA 91404

"In my first interview with a Sierra bear we were frightened and embarrassed, both of us, but the bear's behavior was better than mine." John Muir

Maps

Trail maps vary greatly in accuracy. Many USGS topographic maps are outdated, having been surveyed many years ago, and some were not accurate to begin with. Maps included in trail guides (and virtually all trail guides include some sort of map) can also be imprecise or incorrect (sometimes through no fault of the cartographer—trails can be rerouted from year to year).

In general, you should bear in mind that the map you're using will not be perfect. But imperfect as a map may be, you should never travel in the backcountry without one. Trails can be poorly marked, thick forest or weather conditions can prove disorienting—in short, it is easier to get lost than you realize.

The U.S. Geological Survey has available topographic maps for all the United States. The unit of survey is a quadrangle bounded by parallels of latitude and meridians of longitude, on a scale of either 7½ minutes or 15 minutes. If you know what area you would like to backpack in, you can write the USGS to obtain a free index to topographic mappings of any states. You can then order a specific topo map (costs run about $2.00 per map). Maps of areas east of the Mississippi River and Minnesota should be ordered from: Branch of Distribution, US Geological Survey, 1200 South Eads Street, Arlington VA 22202. For maps of areas west of the Mississippi River, including Louisiana, Alaska and Hawaii, write: Branch of Distribution, US Geological Survey. Box 25286, Federal Center, Denver CO 80225. There are also many authorized dealers of USGS topographic maps, and there may be one in your area. Each state index from the USGS lists the map dealers for that state. Expect to pay more for a USGS map from a private dealer.

Wilderness Press has recently embarked on a project to remap some of the quadrangles of California's High Sierra backcountry. These include the quads of Tuolumne Meadows, Yosemite, Devils Postpile, Fallen Leaf Lake, Mineral King, Hetch Hetchy Reservoir, Merced Peak and Triple Divide Peak, and they far surpass the USGS maps in quality and accuracy. They also publish larger maps to Lassen National Park, Yosemite National Park and Pt. Reyes National Seashore. Write Wilderness Press (see under "Publishers") for a free catalog.

If you are planning to backpack in a national forest, you can usually obtain an inexpensive map of the area from the forest headquarters.

A hiking map of trails throughout New England can be ordered for 50¢ from the New England Trail Conference, 33 Knollwood Dr., East Longmeadow MA 01028.

> "In the eager search for the benefits of modern science and technology, we have been enticed into a nearly fatal illusion: that we have at last escaped from the dependence of man on the balance of nature." Barry Commoner

Trail Guides

Most trail guides have maps and trail descriptions, and many guides include a great deal more, such as chapters on flora, fauna, natural history, geology and other information that will greatly enhance your enjoyment and understanding of what you see along the trails you hike.

In addition to the trail guides we have listed here, there may be a number of sources in the particular area you plan to hike in: Sierra Club chapters and local hiking clubs often publish their own booklets or guides to specific areas in their region, or they can tell you where to find them (see our "Kindred Spirits" section for names and addresses); local backpacking shops, even if they don't carry a full line of trail guides, often carry trail guides that cover the backpackable areas nearby; and National Parks usually have bookstores or the like with maps and guidebooks for sale.

The addresses of the trail-guide publishers are listed in the last section of this book. Bear in mind, however, that many publishers are not set up to respond to a request for a single book from a retail customer. In that event, you may have to special-order the book through a local bookstore. (Note: all Wilderness Press titles *are* available directly from the publisher. Write for a free catalog.)

New England

New England Trails. Issued annually in April; contains detailed reports of current trail and shelter conditions throughout New England; $1.50; New England Trail Conference, 33 Knollwood Dr., East Longmeadow MA 01028.

Hiking Trails in the Northeast, by Henley and Sweet; $7.95; Contemporary Books.

AMC Maine Mountain Guide; $6.95; AMC.

Guide to the Appalachian Trail in Maine; $10.90; order from PATC.

50 Hikes in Maine, by J. Gibson; $8.95; Backcountry Publ.

Fifty More Hikes in Maine, by C. Catlett; $8.95; Backcountry Publications.

Baxter State Park and Katahdin Map and Guide; $3.95; DeLorme.

AMC Trail Guide to Mt. Desert Island and Acadia National Park; $2.50; AMC.

Guide to the Appalachian Trail in N.H. and Vt.; $14.95; order from PATC.

AMC Guide to Mt. Washington and the Presidential Range; $4.95; AMC.

Trail Map and Guide to the White Mountain National Forest; $3.95; DeLorme.

AMC White Mountain Guide; $9.95; AMC.

50 Hikes: White Mountains of New Hampshire, by D. Doan; $8.95; Backcountry Publ.

50 More Hikes: New Hampshire, by D. Doan; $8.95; Backcountry Publ.

50 Hikes: Vermont, by R. Sadlier; $7.95; Backcountry Publ.

Guidebook of the Long Trail; $5.50; order from PATC.

AMC Massachusetts and Rhode Island Trail Guide; $9.95; AMC.

Fifty Hikes in Massachusetts, by Brady and White; $8.95; Backcountry Publ.

50 Hikes: Connecticut, by Hardys; $7.95; Backcountry Publ.

Guide to the Appalachian Trail in N.Y. and N.J.; $5.45; order from PATC.

Guide to the Catskills; $7.95; AMC.

Guide to the Adirondack Trails; $8.75; order from PATC.

Discover the Adirondacks, I, by B. McMartin; $6.95; Backcountry Publ.

Discover the Adirondacks, II, by B. McMartin; $7.95; Backcountry Publ.

Mid-Atlantic

Hiking Trails in the Mid-Atlantic States, by E. Garvey; $6.95; order from PATC.

Pennsylvania Hiking Trails; $3.50; Keystone Trail Assoc.

Official Guide to the Appalachian Trail in Pennsylvania; $2.75; Keystone Trail Assoc.

Fifty Hikes in Eastern Pennsylvania, by C. Hoffman; $8.95; Backcountry Publications.

Fifty Hikes in Western Pennsylvania, by T. Thwaites; $8.95; Backcountry Publications.

Fifty Hikes in Central Pennsylvania, by T. Thwaites; $6.95; Backcountry Publications.

Guide to the Tuscarora Trail; $1.40;
Keystone Trail Assoc.

Hiking Virginia's National Forests, by
K. Wuertz-Schaefer; $6.95; Eastwoods
Press.

*Appalachian Trail Guide to Southern
and Central Virginia;* $12.45; order
from PATC.

*Guide to the Appalachian Trail from
the Susquehanna River to Shenandoah
National Park;* $6.00; order from
PATC.

*PATC Guide to Trails in Shenandoah
National Park;* $11.00; order from
PATC.

Circuit Hikes in Virginia, West Virginia, Maryland and Pennsylvania;
$2.50; order from PATC.

Hiker's Guide for the Big Schloss
[Virginia-West Virginia]; $2.00; order
from PATC.

*Circuit Hikes in Shenandoah National
Park;* $2.50; order from PATC.

*Hiking Guide to the Monongahela
National Forest and Vicinity;* $5.00;
order from PATC.

Cranberry Backcountry [West Virginia]; $2.50; order from PATC.

Southeast

Hiking Trails in the Southern Mountains, by Sullivan and Daniel; $6.95;
Contemporary Books.

*Guide to the Backpacking and Day
Hiking Trails of Kentucky,* by A.
Lander; $9.95; Thomas Press (2030
Ferdon Rd., Ann Arbor MI 48104).

Tennessee Hiking Trails, by E. Means;
$6.95; Eastwoods Press.

*Official Guide to the Appalachian Trail
in Tennessee and North Carolina,
Cherokee, Pisgah and Great Smokies;*
$10.95; order from PATC.

Hiker's Guide to the Smokies, by D.
Murlless and C. Stallings; $8.95; Sierra
Club Books.

100 Favorite Trails of the Great Smokies and the Carolina Blue Ridge; $1.50;
order from PATC.

*Guide to the Appalachian Trail in the
Great Smokies, the Nantahalas, and
Georgia;* $9.95; order from PATC.

North Carolina Hiking Trails, by A.
deHart; $9.95; Appalachian Mountain
Club.

Hiking Trails of North Georgia, by T.
Homan; $6.95; Peachtree Publ. (494
Armor Circle N.E., Atlanta GA 30324).

Florida by Paddle and Pack: 45 Wilderness Trails in Central and South Florida,
by M. Toner; $6.95; Banyan Books
(P.O. Box 431160, Miami FL 33143).

Trails of Alabama; $5.00; Alabama
Environmental Quality Assoc. (3815
Interstate Court, Suite 202, Montgomery AL 36109).

Elephants should not be hunted, since the decoys are
so heavy.   R. E. Gardella

Midwest

Hiking Trails in the Midwest, by Sullivan and Daniel; $7.95; Contemporary Books.

Mid-America Trips and Trails, by B. Thomas; $6.95; Stackpole Books.

Backpacking in Michigan, by P. Allen and G. DeRuiter; $8.95; U. of Michigan Press (P.O. Box 1104, Ann Arbor MI 48106).

Minnesota Walk Book, Vol. 2, by J. Buchanan; $3.95; Nodin Press.

Minnesota Walk Book, Vol. 3, by J. Buchanan; $4.50; Nodin Press.

Minnesota Walk Book, Vol. 4, by J. Buchanan; $4.50; Nodin Press.

Hiking Trails in the Black Hills [South Dakota], by M. Fielder; $2.95; North Plains Press.

Southwest

Hiking and Backpacking Trails of Texas, by M. Little; $6.95; Gulf Pub. (P.O. Box 2609, Houston TX 77001).

Hiker's Guide to Big Bend National Park; $1.25; order from Big Bend Natural History Assoc. (Big Bend National Park, Texas 79834).

Guide to New Mexico Mountains, by H. Ungnade; $5.95; University of New Mexico Press.

Hikers and Climbers Guide to the Sandia Mountains, by M. Hill; $9.95; U. of New Mexico Press.

Arizona Trails, by D. Mazel; $9.95; Wilderness Press.

Arizona's Northland Trails, by G. Bunker; $1.25; La Siesta Press.

A Naturalist's Grand Canyon Hiking Guide, by S. Aitchison; price unknown; Foot Trail Publications (176 Bedford Rd., Greenwich CT 06830).

Hiking the Grand Canyon and Havasupai, by L. Morris; $5.95; Aztex (1126 N. Sixth Ave., P.O. Box 50046, Tucson AZ 85703).

Grand Canyon Treks, by H. Butchart; $2.95; La Siesta Press.

Grand Canyon Treks II, by H. Butchart; $1.95; La Siesta Press.

Oak Creek Canyon and the Red Rock Country of Arizona: A Natural History and Trail Guide, by S. Aitchison; $5.95; order from Bradshaw Color (P.O. Box 195, Sedona AZ 86336).

Mountain

North Idaho Hiking Trails; $6.95; Challenge Expedition Co. (Box 1852, Boise ID 83701).

Fifty Eastern Idaho Hiking Trails, by R. Mitchell; $5.95; Pruett.

Trails of Western Idaho, by M. Fuller; $10.95; Signpost.

Hiking Trails of Southern Idaho, by S. Bluestein; $7.95; Caxton (P.O. Box 700, Caldwell ID 83605).

Hiker's Guide to Glacier National Park, by D. Nelson; $5.95; Tecolote Press.

Trails of the Sawtooth and White Cloud Mountains, by M. Fuller; $8.95; Signpost.

The Sawtooth National Recreation Area, by L. Linkhart; $12.95; Wilderness Press.

Hiking the Great Basin, by J. Hart; $9.95; Sierra Club Books.

Field Book: Yellowstone Park and the Absaroka Range, by O. and L. Bonney; $7.95; Bonney.

Hiking the Teton Backcountry, by P. Lawrence; $5.95; Sierra Club Books.

Hiking the Yellowstone Backcountry, by O. Bach; $8.95; Sierra Club Books.

Exploring Yellowstone, by R. Kirk; $2.95; University of Wash. Press.

Wind River Trails, by F. Mitchell; $3.50; Wasatch Publishers.

Beyond the Tetons, by R. Maughan; $5.95; Pruett.

Field Book: Wind River Range, by O. and L. Bonney; $5.95; Bonney.

Field Book: Big Horn Range, by O. and L. Bonney; $7.95; Bonney.

Field Book: The Teton and Gros Ventre Ranges, by O. and L. Bonney; $7.95; Bonney.

Guide to Grand Teton National Park and Jackson's Hole, by O. and L. Bonney; $3.45; Bonney.

Climbing and Hiking in the Wind River Mountains, by J. Kelsey; $8.95; Sierra Club Books.

Guide to the Continental Divide Trail, Volume I: Northern Montana, by J. Wolfe; $8.95; Continental Divide.

Guide to the Continental Divide Trail, Southern Montana and Idaho, Vol. 2, by J. Wolfe; $8.95; Continental Divide.

Guide to the Continental Divide Trail: Wyoming, Vol. 3, by J. Wolfe; $9.95; Continental Divide.

Guide to the Continental Divide Trail: Northern Colorado, Vol. 4, by J. Wolfe; $9.95; Continental Divide.

Trails of the Front Range, by L. Kenofer; $4.95; Pruett.

Rocky Mountain National Park Hiking Trails, by K. and D. Dannen; $7.95; Eastwoods Press.

Grater's Guide to Zion, Bryce Canyon; $1.00; Binford & Mort.

Rocky Mountain Trails, by L. Kenofer; $4.95; Pruett.

Rocky Mountain National Park Trail Guide, by E. Nilsson; $4.95; World Publications (Box 366, Mountain View CA 94042).

Hiking Trails of Northern Colorado, by M. Hagen; $5.95; Pruett Publishing.

Hiking Trails of the Boulder Mountain Area, by V. DeHaan; $5.95; Pruett Publishing.

80 Northern Colorado Hiking Trails, by D. & R. Lowe; $8.95; Touchstone Press.

50 West Central Colorado Hiking Trails, by D. & R. Lowe; $8.95; Touchstone Press.

Hiking Trails of Southwestern Colorado, by P. Pixler; $5.95; Pruett.

Hiker's Guide to Montana, by B. Schneider; $6.95; Falcon Press.

Hiker's Guide to the Superstition Mountains, by D. Nelson; $4.95; Tecolote Press.

Hiker's Guide to Utah, by D. Hall; $7.95; Falcon Press.

The Hiker's Guide to Utah, by D. Hall; $7.95; Wasatch Publishers.

Canyon Country Hiking [Southeastern Utah], by F. A. Barnes; $4.50; Wasatch Publishers.

Wasatch Trails [nr. Salt Lake], by Bottcher and Davis; $2.00; Wasatch Publishers.

Utah Valley Trails, by Paxman and Taylor; $2.50; Wasatch Publishers.

High Uinta Trails [Northeastern Utah], by M. Davis; $3.50; Wasatch Publishers.

Wasatch Trails, Vol. II, by D. Geery; $2.50; Wasatch Publishers.

Petzoldt's Teton Trails, by P. Petzoldt; $4.00; Wasatch Publishers.

Cache Trails [Cache Valley], by Davis and Schimpf; $2.50; Wasatch Publishers.

Pacific Northwest

Crater Lake National Park, by J. Schaffer; $9.95; Wilderness Press.

60 Hiking Trails, Central Oregon Cascades, by D. & R. Lowe; $8.95; Touchstone Press.

Trails of Badger Creek Area [Oregon]; $4.95; Signpost.

Guide to the Middle and South Santiam Roadless Area; $2.50; Sierra Club, Mary's Peak Group (Box 863, Corvallis OR 97330).

Hiking the Gifford Pinchot Back Country; $2.95; Sierra Club, Columbia Group (2637 SW Water St., Portland OR 97201).

The Pacific Crest Trail, Vol. II: Oregon & Washington, by Schaffer and the Hartlines; $14.95; Wilderness Press.

Up and Down the North Cascades National Park, by A. May; $2.95; Mt. Rainier Natural History Assoc. (Longmire, Wash.).

101 Hikes in the North Cascades, by H. Manning; $7.95; The Mountaineers.

Footsore 1: Walks and Hikes Around Puget Sound, by H. Manning; $6.95; The Mountaineers.

Footsore 2: Walks and Hikes Around Puget Sound, by H. Manning; $6.95; The Mountaineers.

Footsore 3: Walks and Hikes Around Puget Sound, by H. Manning; $6.95; The Mountaineers.

Footsore 4: Walks and Hikes Around Puget Sound, by H. Manning; $6.95; The Mountaineers.

Hiking the Bigfoot Country: The Wildlands of Northern California and Southern Oregon, by J. Hart; $8.95; Sierra Club Books.

Getting Off on 96 and Other Less Travelled Roads, by Bleything and Hawkins; $4.95; Touchstone Press.

Indian Heaven Back Country [Southwest Wash. Cascades], by M. Hansen; $5.95; Touchstone Press.

Exploring the Olympic Peninsula, by R. Kirk; $7.95; University of Wash. Press.

Exploring Mt. Rainier, by R. Kirk; $7.95; University of Wash. Press.

Hiking the North Cascades, by F. T. Darvill, Jr.; $9.95; Sierra Club Books.

102 Hikes in the Alpine Lakes, South Cascades and Olympics, by H. Manning; $7.95; The Mountaineers.

50 Hikes in Mt. Rainier National Park, by H. Manning; $6.95; The Mountaineers.

Roads and Trails of Olympic National Park, by F. Leissler; $7.95; University of Wash. Press.

California

Backpacking Guide to San Diego County, by S. Ruland; price unknown; order from author at 3514 S. Cordoba Ave., Spring Valley CA 92077.

The Pacific Crest Trail, Vol. I: California, by Schaffer et al.; $16.95; Wilderness Press.

The Anza-Borrego Desert Region, by the Lindsays; $7.95; Wilderness Press.

Exploring Joshua Tree, by R. Mitchell; $1.95; La Siesta Press.

San Bernardino Mountain Trails, by J. W. Robinson; $9.95; Wilderness Press.

Trails of the Angeles [San Gabriel Mountains], by J. W. Robinson; $9.95; Wilderness Press.

Self-Propelled in the Southern Sierra Vol. I: The Sierra Crest and the Kern Plateau, by J. C. Jenkins; $11.95; Wilderness Press.

Self-Propelled in the Southern Sierra, Vol. 2: The Great Western Divides, by J. C. Jenkins; $9.95; Wilderness Press.

Sierra South, by Winnett and Winnett; $9.95; Wilderness Press.

Yosemite National Park, by J. Schaffer; $12.95; Wilderness Press.

Yosemite [High Sierra Hiking Guide #1], by B. & M. Pierce; $4.95; Wilderness Press.

Mt. Abbot [High Sierra Hiking Guide #2], by T. Winnett; $4.95; Wilderness Press.

Tuolumne Meadows [High Sierra Hiking Guide #4], by Winnett & Schaffer; $4.95; Wilderness Press.

Mt. Whitney [High Sierra Hiking Guide #5], by T. Winnett; $4.95; Wilderness Press.

Devil's Postpile [High Sierra Hiking Guide #6], by R. Felzer; $4.95; Wilderness Press.

Mineral King [High Sierra Hiking Guide #8], by R. Felzer; $4.95; Wilderness Press.

Mt. Goddard [High Sierra Hiking Guide #10], by J. W. Robinson; $4.95; Wilderness Press.

Merced Peak [High Sierra Hiking Guide #11], by B. and M. Pierce; $4.95; Wilderness Press.

Hetch Hetchy [High Sierra Hiking Guide #12], by R. Felzer; $4.95; Wilderness Press.

Kern Peak-Olancha [High Sierra Hiking Guide #13], by Jenkins & Robinson; $4.95; Wilderness Press.

Silver Lake [High Sierra Hiking Guide #17], by J. Grodin; $4.95; Wilderness Press.

Sonora Pass [High Sierra Hiking Guide #18], by J. Schaffer; $4.95; Wilderness Press.

Pinecrest [High Sierra Hiking Guide #19], by B. Schifrin; $4.95; Wilderness Press.

Triple Divide Peak [High Sierra Hiking Guide #20], by Andrew Selters; $4.95; Wilderness Press

Sierra North, by Winnett and Winnett; $9.95; Wilderness Press.

The Tahoe-Yosemite Trail, by T. Winnett; $5.95; Wilderness Press.

The Tahoe Sierra, by J. Schaffer; $9.95; Wilderness Press.

High Sierra & Mt. Whitney Trails; $1.25; Western Trails Publications.

The John Muir Trail, by T. Winnett; $5.95; Wilderness Press.

Starr's Guide to the John Muir Trail, ed. by D. Robinson; $7.95; Sierra Club Books.

Timberline Country: The Sierra High Route, by S. Roper; $9.95; Sierra Club Books.

The John Muir Trail, by D. and R. Lowe; $7.95; Caxton Press (P.O. Box 700, Caldwell ID 83605).

An Outdoor Guide to the San Francisco Bay Area, by D. Whitnah; $9.95; Wilderness Press.

A Guide to the Golden Gate National Recreation Area, by D. Whitnah; $6.95; Wilderness Press.

Exploring Point Reyes, by P. Arnot; $4.95; Wide World, Inc.

Desolation Wilderness and the South Lake Tahoe Basin, by J. Schaffer; $7.95; Wilderness Press.

Mono Lake Guidebook, by Mono Lake Committee; $5.95; order from Wilderness Press.

Lassen Volcanic National Park, by J. Schaffer; $12.95; Wilderness Press.

Lassen Trails, by S. Matteson; $1.00; order from Loomis Museum Assoc. (Lassen Volcanic National Park, Mineral CA 96063).

Marble Mountain Wilderness, by D. Green; $9.95; Wilderness Press.

The Trinity Alps, by L. Linkhart; $9.95; Wilderness Press.

Point Reyes, by Dorothy Whitnah; $7.95; Wilderness Press

Peninsula Trails, by Jean Rusmore and Frances Spangle; $8.95; Wilderness Press.

South Bay Trails, by Frances Spangle and Jean Rusmore; $8.95; Wilderness Press.

Alaska and Hawaii

Discover Southeast Alaska with Pack and Paddle, by M. Piggott; $7.95; The Mountaineers.

55 Ways to the Wilderness in South-Central Alaska; $7.95; The Mountaineers.

Exploring Katmai National Monument; $11.00; Alaska Travel Books (Suite 312, Park Place Bldg., Seattle WA 98101).

The Milepost [Alaska]; $9.95; Alaska Northwest.

Hawaii's Best Hiking Trails, by R. Smith; $8.95; Wilderness Press.

Hiking Hawaii, by R. Smith; $5.95; Wilderness Press.

Hiking Kauai, by R. Smith; $5.95; Wilderness Press.

Hiking Oahu, by R. Smith; $5.95; Wilderness Press.

Hiking Maui, by R. Smith; $5.95; Wilderness Press.

Hawaiian Hiking Trails, by C. Chisholm; $5.95; Touchstone Press.

Hawaiian Camping, by Shirly Rizzuto; $4.95; Wilderness Press.

"If a person lost would conclude that after all he is not lost, he is not beside himself, but standing in his own old shoes on the very spot where he is, and that for the time being he will live there; but the places that have known him, they are lost . . . how much anxiety and danger would vanish."   Henry David Thoreau

Where To Go

Where to go? We have to confess to being somewhat staggered by the wonderful-sounding parks, forests and wilderness areas that we discovered for the first time when we began researching this question; and also by the mountains of printed matter—brochures, flyers, maps, letters from rangers and supervisors—that descended upon us after we began making inquiries. We discovered how much we could find out simply by writing letters, and that rather than falling into some vast bureaucratic hole called the National Park Service or the U.S. Forest Service, the letters got answered—and often answered by people who knew a lot about the backcountry we were asking about.

What we have tried to give you here is not all the information you need to backpack in a particular area, but rather the *sources* for that complete information, the names and addresses to get you started. *Do not go backpacking in an area simply on the basis of what we have told you.* Write letters, and find out everything you can about the terrain, trail lengths and difficulty, climate, where to get a permit, and anything unusual about the area that you should know about. One suggestion: make your inquiries as early in the season as you can, or during the winter months if possible. The offices involved are so much busier during summer months that you might have to wait longer for a response. But do plan your trip thoughtfully and realistically: you could save yourself a lot of headaches later on (when you might discover, for example, that rain showers are a daily occurrence, or that the trail you chose is uncomfortably crowded).

Here are some facts about the types of backcountry you may be hiking in.

National Parks and National Monuments. All our National Parks and Monuments are administered by the National Park Service within the Department of the Interior. Each park is administered by a Park Superintendent whose headquarters are in the park and who may be contacted for information. There is bus service to all the National Parks, or a nearby city, by Greyhound or Continental Trailways.

Most parks are very busy in the summer, and less crowded during spring and fall months. Parks in the northern states may be snowbound during the winter, but parks in the southern states are open year-round.

National Forests. All National Forests are administered by the U.S. Forest Service within the Department of Agriculture. They are managed on a multiple-use principle, which means they are used not only for hiking, camping and other recreation, but also for logging, mining, watershed management, and grazing. Trails and logging roads, some abandoned and some in use, crisscross most National Forests.

The forest headquarters is usually not in the forest but in a nearby city or town. The forest is divided into districts, each managed by a district ranger, and the forest headquarters can tell you where to find the district ranger of the area you plan to visit. That district ranger can issue you a permit and supply you with information about trails, best campsites, or whatever.

Wilderness and Primitive Areas. Wilderness areas are sections of national forests that have been set aside to insure that they will remain natural and unspoiled. As such, they offer outstanding opportunities for a true wilderness experience. No motorized vehicles are allowed in wilderness areas, and although you will find hiking trails, you will not find any readymade campsites or picnic areas.

Bureau of Land Management lands. The Bureau of Land Management, part of the Dept. of the Interior, manages many millions of acres of public land. Most of the land is completely undeveloped, and has no marked hiking trails.

State Forests and State Parks. These areas vary greatly in size, degree of development and regulation, and suitability for backpacking. We have listed names and addresses of state offices, where you can get information on hiking in state forests and parks, in those states with large tracts of undeveloped state park or, more usually, state forest land; and in those states that offer few other backpacking opportunities.

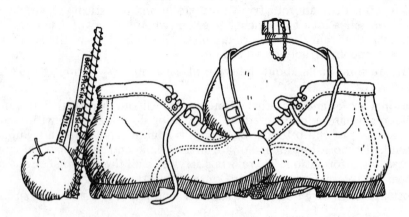

NEW ENGLAND

Maine, New Hampshire, Vermont, Massachusetts, Connecticut, New York

Maine

Acadia National Park (RFD #1, Bar Harbor ME 04609)

The Park was established to preserve the natural beauty of part of Maine's rocky coast, coastal mountains and offshore islands. Most of the Park's 41,642 acres are on Mt. Desert Island which also includes the city of Bar Harbor, other resort communities and fishing villages. Park Loop Road, a 20-mile scenic drive, offers superb views of island-studded Frenchman, Blue Hill and Penobscot bays and the rockbound mainland coast. There are 120 miles of hiking trails and over 40 miles of carriage paths. Visitors should be prepared for a wide variety of weather conditions: Summer 45°F to 85°F, spring and fall 30°F to 70°F. A variety of fishing opportunities are possible from the shorelines of the many lakes and ponds.

There are no overnight accommodations in the Park. Lodging and food may be found in adjacent towns. The Park has two campgrounds.

Because of its small size and the great number of campers, overnight backpacking is not allowed. Those interested in camping at Blackwoods Campground from June 15 to September 5 must make reservations in person or by mail. During the rest of the year Blackwoods is open on a first-come, first-served basis, as is Seawall Campground during the entire summer season. There are also 11 private campgrounds outside of the Park.

State Parks

Most of Maine's state parks are available for day hiking; overnight camping is allowed only at authorized campsites. Entrance fees vary ranging up to $6 per night at certain parks where camping is permitted. Of special interest are:

Baxter State Park A vast 200,000-acre woodland wilderness preserve offering excellent fishing, mountain climbing and 150 miles of trails. Reservations are recommended and must be paid in advance and confirmed. Contact the Reservation Clerk, Baxter State Park Authority, Millinocket ME 04462

Allagash Wilderness Waterway This 200,000-acre preserve in northern Maine offers white-water canoeing within an area that is administered primarily to preserve its wilderness character. Campsites are accessible by boat, the opportunities for backpacking are limited and no reservations are accepted. Write Bureau of Parks and Recreation, State House, Augusta ME 04333 for additional information. They can also supply you with a brochure that gives a brief description of all of Maine's 29 state parks.

New Hampshire

Most backpacking opportunities in New Hampshire are found in the White Mountain National Forest, which covers about 750,000 acres both in New Hampshire and Maine. This Forest's nearness to Boston, New York and Montreal has made it a popular backpacking area, and in some areas regulations have been established to restrict use.

The Presidential Range is probably the best known part of the "White Mountains," but in fact there are hundreds of peaks altogether, with an enormous woodland stretching between mountains and along their slopes. The White Mountains contain the largest alpine zone in the eastern United States, covering eight square miles above timberline, and some of their peaks—particularly Mt. Washington—are famous for sudden and dramatic changes in weather. Generally all areas above timberline fall under the "Restricted Use Area" category, which means overnight camping is not allowed.

In addition to undesignated camp sites, there are many huts, cabins, shelters and campgrounds maintained by the Forest Service, the Appalachian Mountain Club and others. All of the AMC huts require reservations and some shelters require a fee; these facilities are popular, so make reservations far in advance.

Great Gulf Wilderness

A permit is required for the overnight use of these 5,552 acres. Permits during summer months may be reserved no more than 30 days in advance. Write: Androscoggin Ranger District, Gorham NH 03581.

Dry River Wilderness

Fewer restrictions govern the use of this larger (20,280 acres) Wilderness. Permits are not required except for fires. They can be obtained from the AMC at Pinkham Notch and various AMC huts; New Hampshire State Parks at Mt. Washington and Crawford Notch; and in person or by mail from District Rangers in Bethlehem, Gorham, Plymouth and Conway in New Hampshire, in Bethel, Maine, or at the Forest Supervisor's office in Laconia.

National Forest
White Mountain National Forest
P.O. Box 638
Laconia NH 03246

Vermont

There are over 700 miles of hiking trails in Vermont. Of particular note are the Vermont section of the Appalachian Trail and the Long Trail, which winds along the high country of the Green Mountains for more than 250 miles. Because so much of the trail mileage, including that on public land, has been constructed and is largely maintained by private hiking clubs, the hiking clubs are an important source of information about trails, shelters and facilities. Check the "Hiking Clubs" section for names and addresses.

For information on backpacking opportunities on state forest land, contact the State of Vermont Agency of Environmental Conservation, Dept. of Forests, Parks and Recreation, Montpelier VT 05602, (802) 828-3375.

Lye Brook Wilderness
This area contains about 15,538 acres of Green Mountain National Forest land. Most of the area was logged around the turn of the century and there are remnants of railroad grades and old logging roads throughout the area. A large, open, meadow-like area known as "The Burning," caused by fire many years ago, runs along the ridgetop in the southwestern part of the area. Along the old Lye Brook railroad grade lies a deep gorge with a waterfall, believed to be the highest in Vermont. There are no permanent roads providing access to the area. Write the Green Mountain National Forest headquarters for additional information. No permit is required for entry.

Bristol Cliffs Wilderness
The main feature of this 3,775-acre Wilderness is South Mountain, with a 2,325-foot summit. Vegetation is primarily northern hardwoods, and two natural ponds within the area support active beaver colonies. The cliffs and talus slopes of the west escarpment that give this Wilderness its name offer spectacular views of Champlain Valley and the Adirondack Mountains in New York State. There are no developed roads or trails in the Wilderness. Write Green Mountain National Forest headquarters for additional information. No permit is required for entry.

National Forest
Green Mountain National Forest
P.O. Box 519
Rutland VT 05701

Massachusetts

The most notable backpacking opportunities are found on the Massachusetts segment of the Appalachian Trail, which winds along the summits of the Berkshires in the western part of the state. There are also trails and primitive campsites in many state forests and parks. For information and free individual area maps, write Division of Forests and Parks, 100 Cambridge Street, Boston MA 02202, (617) 727-3180.

Cape Cod National Seashore (South Wellfleet MA 02663)

While hiking on the beach at the National Seashore offers a wonderful daylight experience, overnight camping along the trails is not permitted. Most trails are less than 2 miles long, and the longest is about 8 miles. The entire National Seashore is regulated as a day-use area.

Connecticut

There is limited opportunity for backpacking in Connecticut. There are no federally administered forests or wilderness areas here, and while there are 88 Connecticut State Parks and 29 Connecticut State Forests, camping along hiking trails is generally not permitted.

However, trailside camping on state lands in Connecticut is permitted within the vicinity of the five Adirondack shelters located along the Appalachian Trail, which passes through the state. Of these shelters, one is located within the Macedonia Brook State Park in Kent, three are within Mohawk State Park in Cornwall, and one is within Housatonic State Forest in Cornwall. For information on all, write the Department of Environmental Protection, Parks and Recreation Unit, 165 Capitol Ave., Hartford CT 06106.

The other opportunity for trailside camping in Connecticut is at Pachaug State Forest, where use of the one Adirondack shelter and tent-camping within its immediate vicinity is available on a permit basis. Application for a permit should be made to the Eastern District Hdqtrs., Route 66, Marlborough CT 06447, (203) 295-9523.

New York

There are no federally managed lands in New York suitable for backpacking, but there are 146 State Parks, most of which permit backpacking in designated hiking areas. The most popular areas include the Appalachian Trail section in the Palisades and the Taconic State Park regions. Within the Palisades region, Harriman State Park has a chain of trail shelters that will accommodate six to eight people each. These shelters are located about a day's hike apart, and tents may be set up nearby if a shelter is full. No fees are charged for overnight stops. For more information, write Parks & Recreation, Agency Building 1, Empire State Plaza, Albany NY 12238, (518) 474-0456.

In addition, the Forest Preserve in the Adirondacks and the Catskills offers more than 800 miles of trails. The Department of Environmental Conservation publishes a number of maps and pamphlets describing the various trail systems in these regions. These can be obtained free by writing the Department at 50 Wolf Road, Albany NY 12223.

Substantial information on hiking trails in New York is also available from the following trail organizations: Finger Lakes Conference, PO Box 18048, Rochester NY 14618 (Finger Lakes Region); Adirondack Mountain Club, 172 Ridge Street, Glens Falls NY 12801, (518) 793-7737 (northern New York); and New York-New Jersey Trails Conference, 20 West 40th St., New York NY 10018, (212) 921-4025 (southern New York).

MID-ATLANTIC

New Jersey, Pennsylvania, Delaware, Maryland, Virginia, West Virginia

New Jersey

New Jersey has no federally managed public lands suitable for backpacking, but several large state parks and state forests have trails and hike-in campsites. Largest of the state forests are. Lebanon Forest (29,472 acres) near New Lisbon, and Wharton Forest (102,917 acres) near Hammonton. Write the Division of Parks and Forestry, CN 404, Trenton NJ 08625 for complete information on trails and camping areas. Trails of particular interest are the Batona Trail, which cuts through 40 miles of wilderness in both the Lebanon and Wharton forests, and the Appalachian Trail, which passes through two state parks and two state forests, and covers a distance of 66 miles in New Jersey. See the "Hiking Clubs" section for good sources of information about the Appalachian Trail.

Pennsylvania

In addition to backpacking opportunities in the 501,898 acres of Allegheny National Forest in northern Pennsylvania, and along the Pennsylvania stretch of the Appalachian Trail, backpacking is permitted in two million acres of State Forest land without a permit. For information on trails and regulations, contact Commonwealth of Pennsylvania, Dept. of Environmental Resources, P.O. Box 1467, Harrisburg PA 17120.

Delaware Water Gap National Recreation Area (Bushkill PA 18324)
Most of the backpacking here is done on its 25-mile stretch of the Appalachian Trail, for which no permit is required.

National Forest
Allegheny National Forest
Box 847
Warren PA 16365

Delaware

Delaware contains no national parks or forests, and while none of its State Parks has any backpacking trails, some offer short hiking trails and tent-camping areas. For information, write Division of Parks and Recreation, Box 1401, Dover DE 19901.

Maryland

Backpacking is possible in Maryland on both state forest and state park lands. In particular, the two largest state forests, Savage River (53,000 acres) and Green Ridge (28,305 acres), offer the best opportunities, with primitive campsites and a marked backpacking trail. For more information write Department of Natural Resources, 580 Taylor Avenue, Annapolis MD 21401, (301) 269-3776.

Catoctin Mountain Park (Thurmont MD 21788)
Overnight camping is not permitted on the hiking trails of this 5,767-acre mountain park, nor at the adjoining State Park, Cunningham Falls, except at two Adirondack shelters located off the Bridle Trail. There is no charge, and they are available on a first-come, first-served basis. A permit can be obtained at the Park's Visitor Center.

Assateague Island National Seashore (Route 2, Box 294, Berlin MD 21811, [301] 641-1441)
This 37-mile-long barrier island is connected to mainland Maryland by a bridge at the northern tip of the island, and to mainland Virginia by a

bridge at the southern end of the island. The southernmost 17 miles of the island make up the Chincoteague National Wildlife Refuge, which is administered by the US Fish and Wildlife Service.

The island has three hike-in campsites in the Maryland portion. Upon arrival one person in the party must check in and register to obtain a backcountry permit. Between June 15 and Labor Day you are limited to seven nights. From Labor Day to June 15 you are limited to 14 nights per site. Pets are prohibited.

For regulations and additional information contact the Superintendent at the address above or the Virginia District Ranger, Assateague Island National Seashore, Box 33, Chincoteague VA 23336, (804) 336-6577.

Virginia

Shenandoah National Park (Luray VA 22835)

Skyline Drive winds along the crest of this outstanding part of the Blue Ridge Mountains, through hardwood forests and wildflower-dotted meadows, with spectacular vistas of historic Shenandoah Valley and the Piedmont along the way.

There are over 190,000 acres of public land here, and 324 miles of maintained trail (including a 94-mile section of the Appalachian Trail). A backcountry permit is required and can be obtained by mail or in person at Park headquarters, all entrance stations, and all visitor centers. Two days is the backcountry camping limit at a single location.

Six trail cabins for hikers are maintained by the Potomac Appalachian Club. Advance reservations are required, so write them at 1718 N St. NW, Washington, D.C. 20036.

For information on accommodations within the Park, write the ARA-Virginia Sky-line Co., Inc., Box 727, Luray, VA 22835.

James River Face Wilderness

As the James River passes through the Blue Ridge Mountains, the resultant watergap varies in elevation from 650 feet near Snowden to 3073 feet at Highcock Knob. A geologic anticline is exposed in the watergap. Adjacent to the boundary in the river, Balcony Falls is a long, often tumultuous series of rapids. Downstream from the falls the river is wider, being the impounded backwater of the Snowden Dam. Roads serve the periphery of the wilderness, but historically the interior has been considered inaccessible because of the rugged terrain. The land is characterized by steeply sloped ridges with frequent cliffs and bluffs.

No permit is required. Write the Jefferson National Forest headquarters for more information and a map of the area.

National Forests

George Washington National Forest
210 Federal Building, Box 233
Harrisonburg VA 22801
(703) 433-2491

Jefferson National Forest
210 Franklin Road SW
Roanoke VA 24011
(703) 982-6274

West Virginia

Otter Creek Wilderness

This 20,000-acre wilderness, located in Tucker and Randolph counties in the Monongahela National Forest, includes almost the entire drainage areas of Otter Creek and Shavers Lick Run. Wildlife in the area includes black bear, white-tailed deer, wild turkey, grouse, snowshoe hare, cottontail rabbit and birds and snakes of many varieties. Most of the area is forested with second-growth timber. Extensive parts of the area are covered by nearly impenetrable stands of rhododendron, which make travel off trail extremely difficult.

More than 40 miles of trails are maintained. There are two Adirondack-type shelters in the Wilderness, each of which will accommodate six people on a first-come, first-served basis.

The area receives more than 55" of precipitation annually, usually quite evenly distributed through the year. Frost may occur during any month. A wilderness permit is not required. Write the Monongahela National Forest Supervisor at the Elkins address for details.

Dolly Sods Wilderness

This rugged mountainous area is set atop the Allegheny Mountains at the 4,000-foot level, in Tucker and Randolph counties. Like Otter Creek Wilderness, it is in a land of harsh climate, with dense rhododendron, thick second-growth hardwood and spruce stands, bogs, streams, beaver ponds and some open "sod" areas, a local name for pastureland. For more information, contact the Forest Supervisor in Elkins or the Potomac District Ranger in Petersburg WV 26847.

National Forest

Monongahela National Forest
Box 1231
Elkins WV 26241

SOUTHEAST

Kentucky, Tennessee, North Carolina, South Carolina, Georgia, Florida, Alabama, Mississippi, Arkansas, Louisiana

Kentucky

There are backpacking opportunities in Kentucky's State Parks and State Forests, and you can get complete information on areas and trails by writing the Department of Parks, Capital Plaza Tower, Frankfort KY 40601. There is also a 60-mile "North-South Trail" in TVA's Land Between the Lakes in western Kentucky. Contact TVA Land Between the Lakes in Golden Pond KY 42231, (502) 924-5602.

Cumberland Gap National Historical Park (Box 840, Middlesboro KY 40965)

This 20,279-acre Park in Kentucky, Virginia and Tennessee is named for the famous mountain pass on the Wilderness Road, explored by Daniel Boone and later developed into a main artery of the great trans-Allegheny migration for settlement of the Old West. There is a 21-mile Ridge Trail through the Park. Camping is allowed on the trail at designated sites and a camping permit is required.

There is a Wilderness Road campground within the Park. Meals and lodging are available in Middlesboro and Cumberland Gap.

Mammoth Cave National Park (Mammoth Cave KY 42259)

What's it like inside the earth? A visit to Mammoth Cave will let you see for yourself. Over 225 miles of charted passageways plus many other unexplored caves are filled with stalactites, stalagmites, domes, pits and historical and archeological remains. In addition to the caves, there are 52,000 acres of forests to explore. The backcountry trail system is 37 miles long, located north of the Green River. There are also 7 miles of developed trails south of the river. A permit can be obtained at Park Headquarters.

There is a primitive campground in the Park and three campsites in the backcountry. Camping is unrestricted within the flood plain along the Green and Nolin rivers. Food and lodging are available at the Mammoth Cave Hotel. Write National Park Concessions, Inc., Mammoth Cave KY 42259.

Beaver Creek Wilderness

This is an area in the Daniel Boone National Forest whose 4,780 acres are almost completely surrounded by scenic cliffs. The land below the rugged cliffs contains a wide variety of wildflowers and ferns, and some virgin stands of yellow poplar and hemlock. Fishing in boulder-strewn Beaver Creek is permitted, and there are several miles of primitive trails in the Wilderness. No permits are required here, but the ranger at the Somerset District Office (just off U.S. 27 in Somerset) can give you useful information on trails, access and fire use.

Red River Gorge

The Red River Gorge, on the Daniel Boone National Forest, with its unique landscape and more than 50 arches, a wide diversity of vegetative types, and a 34-mile National Recreation Trail, provides a fine setting for backpacking. The ranger at the Stanton District Office (on Highway 15) can provide useful information.

Sheltowee Trace

The Sheltowee Trace is a National Recreation Trail and a component of the National Trail System. It extends for 254 miles in Kentucky and Tennessee, mostly through the Daniel Boone National Forest. The trail bears the name "Sheltowee" (big turtle), which is the name given to Daniel Boone by the Indians. Boone explored much of the country through which the trail passes.

National Forest

Daniel Boone National Forest
100 Vaught Road
Winchester KY 40391
(606) 744-5656

Tennessee

In addition to backpacking opportunities in Great Smoky Mountains National Park and Cherokee National Forest, there are many hundreds of miles of other backpackable trails maintained by the State Forests, State Parks, U.S. Army Corps of Engineers, Tennessee Trails Association and others. For a complete listing of these trails, write Tennessee Department of Conservation, 2611 West End Ave., Nashville TN 37203.

Great Smoky Mountains National Park (Gatlinburg TN 37738)

The Great Smoky Mountains of North Carolina and Tennessee are the majestic climax of the Appalachian Highlands and preserve the finest example of temperate deciduous forest in the world. Along the 6,000-foot crest of these mountains is a spruce-fir forest typical of those of central Canada, 1000 miles to the north. More than 1,400 kinds of flowering plants grow in the Park. Wildflowers and migrating birds attract many visitors in late April and early May. If you intend to hike then, bring warm clothing and be prepared for frequent rainstorms.

July and August are the heaviest rainfall months—bring rain gear and insect repellent.

In fall the days are cool and clear, ideal for hiking. The Park has over 800 miles of trails (including 68 miles of the Appalachian Trail). Backcountry permits are required, and as of October 1978, a new experimental procedure allows backcountry shelters in the park to be reserved up to 30 days in advance. (Backcountry campsites without shelters have been on a reservation system since 1977.) Reservations can be made by mail or phone, but the permit itself, for either a campsite or a shelter, must be picked up in person no earlier than 24 hours before the start of the trip. To reserve a campsite or shelter, write the Park headquarters or call (615) 436-9564.

The Park has seven developed campgrounds and three primitive campgrounds. Hotel accommodations are available at the Wonderland Hotel at Elkmont or at LeConte Lodge (accessible only by trail). To reserve a cabin at LeConte Lodge, write LeConte Lodge, Box 350, Gatlinburg TN 37738, (615) 436-4473.

Cohutta Wilderness. See "Georgia" listing.

Gee Creek Wilderness. No overnight camping is permitted in this small area of the Cherokee National Forest.

Joyce Kilmer-Slickrock Wilderness. See "North Carolina" listing.

National Forest
Cherokee National Forest
2321 NW Ocoee St., Box 400
Cleveland TN 37311
(615) 476-5528

North Carolina

Blue Ridge Parkway (700 Northwestern Bank Building, Asheville NC 28801)
Following the crest of the Blue Ridge Mountains, the Blue Ridge Parkway is an elongated park, and for most of its 470-mile length is very narrow. Most trails are short, and there are only two areas where overnight camping outside developed campgrounds is permitted, Rock Castle Gorge (in Virginia) and Basin Creek (in North Carolina). In both places, camping is restricted to specific areas. Write Park headquarters for more information.

Ellicott Rock Wilderness
See "South Carolina" listing.

Joyce Kilmer-Slickrock Wilderness
This 15,000-acre Wilderness in the Nantahala National Forest includes

mountain streams, a 3,800-acre virgin forest, and panoramic views from ridgetops. No permits are necessary. Write national forests in North Carolina for more information.

Linville Gorge

This 7,575-acre Wilderness is spectacularly beautiful, with steep slopes, curious rock formations and overhanging cliffs. For 12 miles the Gorge encloses the Linville River, which drops 2,000 feet into the valleys below. Permits are required to enter the area and can be obtained up to 30 days in advance from: District Ranger, U.S. Forest Service, Box 514, Marion NC, (704) 652-4841.

Shining Rock

This 13,350-acre area was named for the huge quartz-rock outcrops that cap Shining Rock Mountain at a 6,000-foot elevation. It is in one of the southernmost extensions of the vegetative zone called the Canadian Zone, and boasts spruce, fir, hemlock and Appalachian hardwoods. Trails go into much of the area and are heavily used. Permits are required and can be obtained free from the Ranger Station in Pisgah Forest or from the Supervisor's office in Asheville.

National Forests

National Forests in North Carolina (Croatan, Nantahala, Pisgah and Uwharrie)
50 S. French Broad Ave.
Box 2750
Asheville NC 28802
(704) 258-2850, Ext. 348

South Carolina

In addition to backpacking opportunities on the half million acres of the Francis Marion and Sumter national forests, there are some state parks that offer trails and primitive camping. For a descriptive brochure listing all the state parks, write Department of Parks, Recreation and Tourism, Box 71, Columbia SC 29202.

Ellicott Rock Wilderness

This 3,600-acre Wilderness Area is located at the juncture of South Carolina, North Carolina and Georgia. Elevations range from 2100' to 3200'. The area is completely forested with oak, poplar, hemlock and pine vegetation. The 11-mile trail system generally follows the Chattooga River and the East Fork of the Chattooga River. Backpacking during spring and summer weekends is very heavy in this area, with most use concentrated along the river. No permits are necessary. For more information, write the District Ranger at Star Route, Walhalla SC 29691, or the National Forests headquarters.

Wambaw Swamp, Little Wambaw Swamp, Hell Hole Bay and Wambaw Creek Wildernesses

These newly-designated Wildernesses range in size from 1900 acres to 4850 acres. They are wet and swamplike, as the names suggest, and are more suitable for canoeing and walk-in exploring than backbacking. Because of the ferocity of mosquitoes in summer, winter months are best. No permits are required. Contact the Forest Supervisor of Francis Marion National Forest for more information.

National Forests

Forest Supervisor
Francis Marion-Sumter National Forests
Box 970
Columbia SC 29202
(803) 765-5222

Georgia

Cumberland Island National Seashore (Box 806, St. Marys GA 31558)

This barrier island off the coast of Georgia is accessible only by a ferry that makes two runs daily. The island is 16 miles long and three miles wide at its widest point. Forests in the central part of the island support deer, squirrels and raccoons. The beach offers fishing, swimming and shelling. No vehicles are allowed on the island.

The island has a 16-site developed campground and three primitive backcountry sites. Sites at the developed campground must be reserved in advance, the backcountry sites are available on a first-come, first-served basis. In any event you must have confirmed reservations for the ferry that will take you to and from the island. For ferry and campground reservations contact the Superintendent, Box 806, St. Marys GA 31558, (912) 882-4335. Backcountry permits are required for overnight stays.

Cohutta Wilderness

This whole Wilderness totals 34,102 acres; 32,307 acres are located in the Chattahoochee National Forest in north-central Georgia. The remaining 1,795 acres are part of the Cherokee National Forest in southern Tennessee. The Wilderness, noted for its inaccessibility, lies within the Blue Ridge Mountain Range, and features the headwaters of the Conasauga and portions of the Jacks River drainage. Visitors may hunt, fish or enjoy hiking the trails along the two rivers. No permits are required. Write either National Forest for additional information.

Ellicott Rock Wilderness

For a description of this Wilderness Area please see our South Carolina listing.

State Parks

Because of the "approach trail" within the Amicalola Falls State Park to the last part of the Appalachian Trail on Springer Mountain, overnight backpackers can be accommodated in this state park. Backpackers should stop at the Visitor Center to obtain a parking permit and a camping permit if camping overnight in the park. Amicalola Falls State Park, Star Route, Dawsonville GA 30534.

National Forests

Chattahoochee-Oconee National Forests
601 Broad St. NE
Gainesville GA 30501
(404) 536-0541

Florida

Everglades National Park (Box 279, Homestead FL 33030)

The Park encompasses 1,400,533 acres; it is primarily a water park. Fresh water six inches deep and 50 miles wide creeps seaward on a "riverbed" that slopes just centimeters per mile. The Park abounds with wildlife, it is best known, though, for its abundance and variety of birds.

The uniform climate of the Park makes it a year-round attraction, but there are two distinct seasons: summer is wet and winter is dry. There are intense storms from late May through October. Warm, humid conditions bring abundant insects. Summer's high-water levels enable animals to range throughout the Park, so you will not then see the concentration of wildlife so typical of winter months. The 99-mile Wilderness Waterway Trail is a prime attraction; it takes 7–10 days for this trip one-way by canoe. (Winter trips are recommended.)

Motel and housekeeping units are available in the Park. For reservations and rates contact Everglades Park Catering Inc., Flamingo FL 33030, (813) 695-3101. Gas, groceries, laundry, ice, boat and canoe rental are available in the Park at the Flamingo Marina. Accommodations and services are also available outside the Park in nearby Homestead and Everglades City.

Backcountry permits are required and may be obtained at Park Headquarters or a ranger station. There is no reservation system for the backcountry sites located along the waterways.

Big Cypress National Preserve (Box 110, Ochopee FL 33943)

There is only one maintained hiking trail within the preserve: the southernmost section of the Florida Trail, a 29.7-mile trail connecting two state highways. The trail is primarily used during the dry-season months of December through May. There are a variety of designated camping areas which provide well water and dry overnight camping, but the majority of the trail length is remote swampland environment. Land acquisition for the Preserve is still in progress, so there are many areas through which the trail passes that remain in private ownership. The Florida Trail Organization, Box 13708, Gainesville FL 32604, can advise users about the correct procedures and trail regulations.

The rest of the public lands within the preserve are open to unrestricted foot travel; however, there are very few areas with definite trails or paths.

Bradwell Wilderness

This 23,432-acre area is located in Apalachicola National Forest in northwest Florida, about 25 miles southwest of Tallahassee. Hardwood swamps, thick titi swamps and scattered small ponds with either open water or covered by aquatic weeds typify the area. The topography of the area is flat, with the water table very close to the ground surface. Only experienced hikers should attempt an excursion into the core of this wilderness, where there are no trails or identifiable landmarks. Permits are not required. For additional information contact the District Ranger, Forest Service, Box 68, Crawfordville FL 32327, (904) 926-3561.

State Parks

There are 11 state parks in Florida where backpacking and primitive camping can be enjoyed. The parks are administered by the Department of Natural Resources, 3900 Commonwealth Blvd., Tallahassee FL 32304. Two of the parks are:

Torreya State Park. The steep bluffs and deep ravines of this park are reminiscent of the Appalachian Mountains. Nowhere else in Florida can such rugged topography be found or such sharp contrast between high bluffs and flat river swamps.

The Park has two primitive campsites. Hikers must register and obtain parking instructions before camping.

T.H. Stone Memorial/St. Joseph Peninsula State Park. Some of the largest and most impressive sand dunes in the state are found in this 1,650-acre preserve. Primitive camping is permitted in any part of the preserve except on sand dunes and in the sand-pine scrub. All backpackers must register before entering the preserve; there is a capacity limit of 10 persons per day or one group of up to 20 persons per day. The preserve has no facilities. Besides obtaining information from the Department of Natural Resources in Tallahassee, one may also contact the Park Superintendent, Box 909, Port St. Joe FL 32456.

National Forests

Apalachicola-Ocala-Osceola National Forests
2586 Sea Gate Dr., P.O. Box 13549
Turner Bldg., Suite 200
Tallahassee FL 32308
(904) 878-1131

Alabama

National Forests
National Forests in Alabama
1765 Highland Ave.
Montgomery AL 36107
(205) 832-7630

Mississippi

National Forests
Bienville-Delta-DeSoto-Holly Springs-Homochitto-Tombigbee National
Forests
Box 1291
Jackson MS 39205

Arkansas

Upper Buffalo Wilderness
This land totals 10,590 acres and generally includes the headwaters of
the Buffalo River in the southwestern corner of Newton County,
Arkansas. The wilderness is managed by Ozark National Forest and a
backpacking permit is not required. Since no trails have been established
in this area, and there are no bridges across streams, a good system is to
follow a side branch down to the river, then travel up or down the river
to another side branch which leads out. The District Ranger has some
tips on backpacking in this wilderness, and he can be contacted at Box
427, Jasper AR 72641, (501) 446-5122.

Caney Creek Wilderness
These 14,433 acres, managed by Ouachita National Forest, are characterized by year-round clear streams, picturesque rock outcroppings, and
sharp ridges that afford outstanding panoramic views. There are some
short trails and one long trail in the area, and a backcountry permit is
not required. The District Ranger is at 507 Mena Street, Mena AR
71953.

National Forests

Ouachita National Forest   St. Francis National Forest
Box 1270   Box 1008
Hot Springs National Park AR 71901   Russellville AR 72801
(501) 321-5202   (501) 968-2354

Ozark National Forest
Box 1008
Russellville AR 72801
(501) 968-2354

Louisiana

Chicot State Park (Box 494, Ville Platte LA 70586)
In addition to backpacking opportunities in the half-million acres of Kisatchie National Forest, Chicot State Park, which contains 6840 acres of rolling hills and water in south-central Louisiana, maintains a backpacking trail. A permit, required for all overnight backcountry use, can be obtained in person at the Park entrance station or by writing to the Park. There is a permit fee of 25¢ per night.

Kisatchie Hills Wilderness
The Kisatchie National Forest manages these 8,700 acres of exceptionally rugged hills for the State of Louisiana. Several mesas, buttes and sandstone outcrops are lightly covered with stands of longleaf pine and yaupon. The hills, ranging from 120–400 feet in elevation, are known to contain fossils and petrified wood. The Wilderness does not provide a designated trail system at this time, but an existing network of old logging roads offers good access to the various scenic attractions of the Kisatchie Hills. For more information contact the District Ranger at P.O. Box 2128, Natchitoches, LA 71457.

Wild Azalea Trail
This 31-mile trail exposes the hiker to all six vegetation types present on the Kisatchie National Forest. Early to mid spring is the most popular time to hike the trail. At this time, one can experience all the wild azaleas blooming in their natural setting. Many opportunities exist for camping along the trail. Valentine Lake, at the trailhead, also provides swimming and picnicking facilities. The District Ranger is located at 3727 Government Street, Alexandria LA 71301 for further information.

National Forest
Kisatchie National Forest
2500 Shreveport Hwy
Pineville LA 71360
(318) 473-7160

MIDWEST

Ohio, Indiana, Illinois, Michigan, Wisconsin, Minnesota, Iowa, Missouri, Nebraska, South Dakota, North Dakota

Ohio

Besides backpacking opportunities in Wayne National Forest, Ohio has two state forests with trails suitable for overnight hiking. Shawnee State Forest (Portsmouth OH 45662, (614) 858-4201), also called "The Little Smokies of Ohio," offers 60,000 acres of rugged, hilly forest, with over 100 miles of marked trails. Zaleski State Forest (Zaleski OH 45698, [614] 596-5781) offers a 20-mile backpacking trail with historic as well as scenic features. In both forests, a permit is required, and camping is allowed at designated campsites only. Contact forest headquarters for more information.

National Forest
Wayne National Forest
1615 J Street
Bedford IN 47421

Indiana

For specific information on where to hike and backpack in Indiana, the "Indiana Hiking Guide" is available for $3 (including tax and mailing) from: Streams and Trails Section, Division of Outdoor Recreation, Dept. of Natural Resources, 616 State Office Building, Indianapolis IN 46204. It includes detailed maps of trails in Indiana's largest State Park and five largest State Forests. It also provides information on all other state lands and on Hoosier National Forest, Indiana Dunes National Lakeshore and Muscatatuck National Wildlife Refuge. Free maps of the 57-mile Knobstone Trail and surrounding rugged backcountry are also available.

National Forest
Hoosier National Forest
1615 J Street
Bedford IN 47421

Illinois

Of particular interest to backpackers in Illinois is the Ozark-Shawnee Trail, which runs a 115-mile course from Battery Rock on the Ohio River to Grand Tower on the Mississippi. Much of the trail runs through Shawnee National Forest, and campsites are interspersed throughout. The Shawnee National Forest headquarters can supply details.

National Forest
Shawnee National Forest
317 E. Poplar St.
Harrisburg IL 62946

Michigan

Isle Royale National Park (Box 27, Houghton MI 49931)
This Park is a 45-mile-long wilderness archipelago in Lake Superior, accessible only by boat or floatplane. It is a roadless land of wild creatures, evergreen and hardwood forests, lakes and scenic shores. The Park has more than 160 miles of foot trails, and cross-country travel is discouraged because of numerous boggy areas and dense vegetation.

The Park is open to visitors from about mid-May to late October. The National Park Service makes available boat service for the 15-mile trip from Houghton, on the mainland, to Isle Royale. Write the Park Superintendent for rates, schedules and reservations.

All campers, hikers and those travelling in their own boats must register for a permit when they arrive at the Park. Lodge rooms and housekeeping cabins can be reserved by writing: Rock Harbor Lodge, Isle Royale National Park, Houghton MI 49940, (906) 337-4993. Out of season write to National Park Concessions, Mammoth Cave KY 42259, (502) 758-2217.

Pictured Rocks National Lakeshore (Munising, MI 49862)
Along a 15-mile section of the Lake Superior shoreline are multicolored sandstone cliffs of the Pictured Rocks escarpment, which rises abruptly as much as 200 feet above the lake level. In addition to these sandstone cliffs there are broad beaches, sand bars, dunes, waterfalls, inland lakes, ponds, marshes, and hardwood and coniferous forests.

Summer weather is usually pleasant, but hikers should be prepared for cold, rainy weather. Bears and insects can be a nuisance.

A permit is required for backcountry camping, and along the Lakeshore Trail camping is permitted at marked sites only. Hiking opportunities are almost unlimited because of a vast network of old logging roads and trails, but few of these roads and trails are marked, so an adequate map and compass are essential. (A $2.75 topographic map can be ordered from the Eastern National Park and Monument Association, Pictured Rocks National Park, Box 40, Munising MI 49862.)

Sleeping Bear Dunes National Lakeshore (400 Main Street, Frankfort, MI 49635)

Beaches, massive sand dunes, forests and lakes are the outstanding characteristics of these two offshore islands and a section of Lake Michigan shoreline. This National Lakeshore now contains some 68,000 acres.

Backpacking is permitted on South Manitou Island, an eight-square-mile, 5,260-acre island with 12 miles of shoreline. Permits are required and are available from Rangers on the island and the ferry service operator. The only public transportation to the island is provided by the Manitou Mail Service, Leland MI 49654, (616) 256-9116. Although there is no reservation system in effect for campsites on South Manitou, reservations should be made for the ferry ride to the island.

Backpacking is also permitted at the White Pine Campground, located along the 12-mile Platte Plains Trail system and only 1½ miles from the nearest trailhead. A free permit is required.

National Forests

Ottawa National Forest
U.S. 2 East
Ironwood MI 49938

Manistee National Forest
421 S. Mitchell St.
Cadillac MI 49601

Hiawatha National Forest
2727 N. Lincoln Road
Escanaba MI 49829

Huron National Forest
421 S. Mitchell St.
Cadillac MI 49601

Wisconsin

Besides two large national forests and three wilderness areas (two of them created in late 1978), Wisconsin has eight state forests with almost 450,000 acres of backpackable land. Those most highly recommended are the Black River, Brule River, Flambeau River, Northern Kettle Moraine and Northern Highland-American Legion state forests. A permit is required to camp on state forest land, and a use fee is charged at some locations. For more information, contact the Department of Natural Resources, Box 7921, Madison WI 53707.

Rainbow Lake Wilderness

This 6,583-acre portion of the Chequamegon National Forest offers a network of trails passing through rolling, glaciated lake country terrain. There are 15 undeveloped lakes five acres or larger and nine smaller ponds within the wilderness. A 6-mile section of the North Country Trail traverses the area, and old logging roads provide access to other parts of the wilderness. For more information contact the district ranger in Washburn, (715) 373-2667.

Whisker Lake Wilderness
This area of 7,428 acres is located in Florence County, in northeastern Wisconsin, in the Nicolet National Forest. The topography is rolling, with a series of ridges, which is characteristic of glaciated areas. Along the northern boundary flows the Brule River, popular as a canoe stream and for trout fishing. Gravel roads exist in the wilderness and provide nonmotorized access to several small lakes. This wilderness was created in October 1978. For information contact Nicolet National Forest.

Blackjack Springs Wilderness
This Wilderness of 5,886 acres is located in Vilas County in the Nicolet National Forest. The main feature is the Blackjack Springs themselves, the outlet from which flows eventually into the Deerskin River. This river, which forms the north boundary of the wilderness, is a favorite fishing area for trout fishermen. For information on backpacking in this new wilderness, contact Nicolet National Forest.

National Forests

Chequamegon National Forest	Nicolet National Forest
Federal Building	Federal Building
Park Falls WI 54552	Rhinelander WI 54501

Minnesota

Voyageurs National Park (Drawer 50, International Falls MN 56649)
The 219,000 acres of this Park, a vast network of northern lakes surrounded by forest, stretch along the U.S.-Canadian border east of International Falls. Voyageurs is a new Park with visitor facilities in the early stages of development.

There are no roads into the interior of the Park. Travel within the Park is and will remain primarily by boat. A trail system is being planned and developed for both summer and winter use. Chances to hear loons and wolves on overnight trips are highlights of the 10-mile-long Cruiser Lake Trail, which crosses the midsection of the park over recently glaciated bedrock outcrops and through boreal forests. The 1.5-mile Locator Lake Trail gives canoe-portage access to a series of four interconnected interior lakes. Cross-country hikes to other interior lakes are for those with map and compass experience. Access to trailheads is only by boat.

Grand Portage National Monument (Box 666, Grand Marais MN 55604)
This nine-mile portage was a rendezvous for traders and trappers on a principal route of Indians, explorers, missionaries and fur traders into the Northwest. Backpacking is allowed along the Grand Portage Trail, which winds 8.5 miles through the woods from the reconstructed North

West Co. Stockade on Lake Superior to the site of Fort Charlotte on the Pigeon River. The National Park Service cautions you to be prepared for the same discomforts which the voyageurs faced 200 years ago--rocks, wet-slippery terrain, mud, mosquitoes and black flies. Camping is permitted only at the primitive campsites at Fort Charlotte, and a backcountry permit must be obtained first from a Park Ranger.

Boundary Waters Canoe Area

The BWCA is unique in the National Forest Wilderness System—it is the *only* lakeland wilderness. This rocky and lush section of the Superior National Forest supports a labyrinth of streams and rivers and over 1,000 lakes, and is a canoeist's paradise. All hikers and canoeists must obtain a travel permit to enter the BWCA. Ranger stations of the Superior National Forest are located in Cook, Ely, Isabella, Tofte and Grand Marais.

National Forests

Superior National Forest
Box 338
Duluth MN 55801
(218) 727-6692

Chippewa National Forest
Cass Lake MN 56633
(218) 335-2226

Iowa

There are no public lands administered by the federal government in Iowa, but there are two state forests that offer backpacking opportunities.

Yellow River State Forest (Box 115, McGregor IA 52157)

This 5,800-acre forest is located in the midst of spectacular bluffs along the Mississippi River in northeastern Iowa. Of primary backpacking interest is the Paint Creek Unit, a 4,600-acre timbered area with sheer limestone cliffs and clear trout streams. There are several trails within it, and camping is allowed at designated areas only (for a maximum of two weeks).

Stephens State Forest (Route 3, Chariton IA 50049)

These 9,202 forested acres in south-central Iowa are divided into six separate units. The Cedar Creek, Chariton, 1000 Acre and Unionville units are primitive and undeveloped, while there are many miles of trails and roads available in the Lucas and Whitebreast units. In addition, two special backpacking trails have been established and marked southwest of the Whitebreast Unit. The trails are each long enough to provide a two- or three-hour hike each way, and five campsites are provided for overnight camping.

Missouri

In addition to hiking opportunities in the Mark Twain National Forest, there are backpackable trails in some Missouri State Parks. For details write the Missouri Dept. of Natural Resources, Box 176, Jefferson City MO 65102. The Department of Natural Resources is also coordinating efforts to develop a single north-south route, called the Ozark Trail, that will cover 500 miles between St. Louis and western Arkansas. Approximately 180 miles—80 in Missouri and 100 in Arkansas' Ozark N.F.—are now completed.

Hercules Glades Wilderness

This 12,000-acre section of the Mark Twain National Forest offers a combination of open grassland and forested knobs and valleys that create a scenic and unusual terrain. Because the Ozark climate is mild enough to make backpacking feasible throughout the year, as long as you have proper gear, you may want to take advantage of this opportunity and plan your visit outside the peak spring and fall use seasons. A permit is not required.

Bell Mountain Wilderness

This is a rugged area of 8,530 acres in the St. Francois Mountains west of Ironton. The Wilderness is characterized by steep felsite and rhyolite outcroppings, and elevations range from 970 feet in the Joe's Creek drainage to 1,702 feet at Bell Mountain. For more information, contact the District Ranger in Potosi (phone 314-438-5427).

Rock Pile Mountain Wilderness

This 3,920-acre Wilderness is located southwest of Fredericktown. The area is primarily a broken ridge, having steep, rocky slopes running from Little Grass Mountain on the north to the National Forest boundary four miles to the south. For further details contact the District Ranger in Fredericktown (phone 314-783-2790).

Piney Creek Wilderness

This 8,400-acre Wilderness is located in southwestern Missouri's Barry and Stone counties. The area is deeply dissected, with narrow ridgetops separated from narrow hollows by long, steep slopes. Here the endangered bald eagle finds shelter in winter, and a significant colony of blue heron calls it home. For more information contact the District Ranger in Cassville (phone 417-847-2144).

Devil's Backbone Wilderness

This 6,800-acre area, with its narrow ridges and hollows separated by long, steep slopes or bluffs, lies in Ozark County in south-central Missouri. The North Fork of the White River flows through the area for about 1½ miles and provides a good stream fishery of Ozark species. To find out more, contact the District Ranger in Willow Springs (phone 417-469-3155).

National Forests
Mark Twain National Forest
Box 937
Rolla MO 65401
(314) 364-4621

Nebraska

For information on backpacking trails in Nebraska, you can write to:
Nebraska Game and Parks Commission, Box 30370, Lincoln NE 68503.
They will suggest two sections of the Nebraska National Forests and
two state parks as the best areas for backpacking. You can also contact
the Nebraska National Forest Headquarters at 270 Pine St., Chadron NE
69337, (308) 432-3367, for additional details. Here are the areas the
Nebraska Game and Parks Commission suggests:

Valentine National Wildlife Refuge (Valentine NE 69201)

These 71,500 acres offer a setting of natural lakes, marshes, lush meadows and sandhills. Most of the refuge is open to backpacking although
there are no formal trails as such. Since the treeless sandhills can become
scorching hot during summer months, most hikers will prefer to plan
trips during spring and fall. Overnight camping is not allowed on the
refuge, so routes should be designed to end on one of the two adjacent
state primitive camping areas.

National Forests

The Bessey Division of the Nebraska National Forest offers 90,000
acres of prairie and forest, wedged between the Middle Loup and
Dismal rivers. Occasionally periods of fire hazard require a complete
ban on any form of camping. Call ahead to confirm that camping is
being allowed, and register at the Halsey Ranger Station to learn
current conditions.

Soldier Creek Wood Reserve offers the closest thing to traditional
"mountain" backpacking in Nebraska, with 10,000 acres of forested
buttes and canyons. There are over 50 miles of marked trails, and
excellent trout fishing in Soldier Creek.

State Parks

Indian Cave State Park, north of Falls City, has Nebraska's only hardwood forest and is very well developed for backpackers, with well-
marked trails and eight shelters as well as remote campsites. Camping is
allowed in designated campsites only. This is a popular, heavy-use area.
You are required to check in at Park Headquarters before hiking.

South Dakota

Black Elk Wilderness
These 10,700 acres are administered by the Black Hills National Forest. The terrain is rocky and hilly, and is crisscrossed by approximately 58 miles of trails. No permit is required. Contact the Forest Supervisor for more details.

State Parks
Although all of South Dakota's State Parks offer some type of hiking opportunity, only Custer State Park offers a true backpacking experience. The Park features an outstanding cross section of the Black Hills topography. Elevations range from 3,700' to 6,800'. Three major streams cross the Park from west to east. The Park has four man-made lakes, which have been stocked with brown and rainbow trout.

The Park has seven campgrounds as well as two primitive camping areas, which are located in the French Creek Natural Area. The Park also offers lodging in cabins and motels.

Backpackers using the French Creek Natural Area are asked to register at the Visitor Center in the Park. For additional information contact South Dakota Game, Fish & Parks, Division of Custer State Park, Custer SD 57730.

National Forest
Black Hills National Forest
Box 792
Custer SD 57730
(605) 673-2251

North Dakota

Theodore Roosevelt National Memorial Park (Medora ND 58645. 701-623-4466)
This Park offers one of the few backpacking opportunities on public land in North Dakota. These 110 square miles of rugged badlands country, with a seemingly infinite variety of buttes, tablelands, valleys and gorges, are administered by the National Park Service.

The trail system is still under development, and marking and mapping of the trails are incomplete. Hikers are not restricted to existing trails. When you register with a Park Ranger before heading for the backcountry, you can get tips on trail locations, camping spots, etc. General hiking information and topo maps can be obtained at the Visitor Center or Ranger Station.

Little Missouri Bay State Park (c/o North Dakota Parks and Recreation Dept., Box 700, Bismarck ND 58501)
This 6,000-acre primitive park located in the badlands is suitable for backpacking. No permits or fees are required, and a seasonal staff is on hand at the Park to provide necessary information and visitor services.

SOUTHWEST

Oklahoma, Texas, New Mexico, Arizona

Oklahoma

Write to the Oklahoma Tourism and Recreation Department, 500 Will Rogers Building, Oklahoma City OK 73105, (405) 521-2406, for a pamphlet describing all trails—short and long—in the state. In addition, topo maps for all Oklahoma trails can be obtained at Oklahoma Geological Survey, 830 Van Vleet Oval, Norman OK 73069.

Ouachita National Forest (Box 1270, Hot Springs National Park AR 71901)
The headquarters of this 1½-million-acre National Forest is in Arkansas, but there are three ranger districts in Oklahoma: the Choctaw Ranger District in Heavener, the Kiamichi Ranger District in Talihina, and the Taik Ranger District in Idabel. Over 40 miles of trails have been established in the Oklahoma part of the forest.

Texas

According to the Texas Parks and Wildlife Department, there are 540 miles of backpackable trails in Texas, mostly administered by the National Park Service, the Texas Parks and Wildlife Department, the US Forest Service and the US Army Corps of Engineers. The Department (4200 Smith School Road, Austin TX 78744) will send you a listing called "Trails in Texas."

In addition, there is under development the Big Thicket National Preserve (Box 7408, Beaumont TX 77706), 84,550 acres of Big Thicket country in southeastern Texas. The Big Thicket wilderness has been called the "biological crossroads of America"—within its boundaries are temperate and subtropical habitats of jungle, swamp, woodland, plain and desert. Since the National Park Service is still in the land-acquisitions stage, visitor opportunities are limited and camping is allowed only in some units with no trails.

Big Bend National Park (Big Bend National Park TX 79834)
The spectacular canyons of the Rio Grande are this Park's principal attractions. For 107 twisting miles, the river defines the southern boundary of the 730,000-acre Park. Also within the Park are the Chisos Mountains, rising 6,000' above the floodplains and surrounded by the Great Chihuahuan Desert.

The Park has 220 miles of trails and is open year-round. June and July are the hottest months, with average highs of 95° (although along the river temperatures often exceed 100°). July through September is the rainy season, with flash flooding possible, and December through February are the cold months, with highs averaging 64° and lows about 36°. Backcountry permits, required for overnight backpacking, can be obtained at any ranger station or at Park headquarters.

Overnight lodging for 150 guests is available at Chisos Mountain Lodge. Reservations should be made well in advance. Write National Park Concessioners, Inc., Big Bend National Park TX 79834.

Guadalupe Mountain National Park (3225 National Parks Hwy, Carlsbad NM 88220)
The Guadalupe Mountain Range is a massive V-shaped land wedge rising in Texas whose arms reach northward into New Mexico. At its "V" stands El Capitan, a 2000-foot sheer cliff. The mountains and canyons here shelter unique remnants of forest plants and animals which have struggled for survival since the end of the Ice Ages about 10,000 years ago. The Park lies astride these mountains' most scenic and rugged portions.

There are 63 miles of trails in this Park, in varying condition. Facilities and staffing are limited, weather is changeable, and mountain trails are steep and rough. Backcountry users should be prepared to rough it.

Limited camping facilities are available in the Park at the Pine Canyon Campground and Dog Canyon Campground. For backcountry use, a free permit is required and can be obtained at the Information Station. Camping is allowed only in designated areas.

National Forests
The four national forests in Texas—Angelina, Davy Crockett, Sabine and Sam Houston—are clustered near one another in the eastern part of the state and are managed by a central office in Lufkin. For details write the Supervisor's Office, Box 969, Lufkin TX 75901, (409) 632-4446.

Of particular interest in Texas' National Forests is the Lone Star Hiking Trail, which extends 140 miles across the length of the Sam Houston

National Forest. There are two developed campgrounds along the trail, Stubblefield and Double Lake, and primitive camping along the trail is allowed year-round except during hunting season. No permits are required.

New Mexico

New Mexico, with more than 22 million acres of public land, offers almost unlimited backpacking opportunities. More than two thirds of the state is dominated by mountains that range up to 13,161'. All or part of the five national forests have slopes blanketed with pine, aspen, spruce and fir. The eastern third of the state is a high plateau more than 3,000 feet in elevation.

In addition to national park, national monument and national forest land, all the 13 million acres of public land managed by the Bureau of Land Management are available for backpacking. Most of the acreage is usable year-round, although there are no developed or marked hiking trails except for about 10 miles in the Organ Mountains. More desirable BLM areas include the Rio Grande Wild River in Taos County, the Organ Mountains in Dona Ana County, the Hatchet Mountains in Hidalgo County, the Ladron Mountains in Socorro County, and the Florida Mountains in Luna County. To find out more or to purchase detailed maps of these areas, contact the Bureau of Land Management, New Mexico State Office, Box 1449, Santa Fe NM 87501.

Camping on Indian lands is primarily at developed campsites. For more information, contact any of these three tribes: Navajo Tribe, Parks and Recreation Dept., Box 709, Window Rock AZ 86515; Mescalero Apache Tribe, Mescalero NM 88340; and Jicarilla Apache Tribe, Box 147, Dulce NM 87528.

The New Mexico State Parks also offer camping opportunities, although mostly in developed areas. For details, write New Mexico State Park and Recreation Commission, Box 1147, Santa Fe NM 87503.

Guadalupe Mountain National Park (3225 National Parks Hwy, Carlsbad NM 88220)

See under "Texas" listing.

Carlsbad Caverns National Park (3225 National Parks Hwy, Carlsbad NM 88220)

Carlsbad Caverns are on the northeastern slope of the Guadalupe Mountains. On the surface the land is harsh and rugged; below ground, huge galleries decorated with delicate stone formations are always cool and moist.

There are 35 miles of trail in the Park, and backcountry use is limited only by the amount of water hikers are able to carry. Summers are

warm and winters mild, but sudden changes can occur. Spring brings strong winds and summer brings thunderstorms that can cause flash floods.
There are no camping facilities or overnight accommodations in the Park. A backcountry permit is required and can be obtained at the Visitors Center. Entering backcountry caves without written permission of the Park Superintendent is prohibited.

Bandelier National Monument (Los Alamos NM 87544)

This beautiful canyon country contains many cliff and open pueblo ruins of the late prehistoric period. Backpacking is popular on Bandelier's 32,737 acres, although certain areas of archeological ruins are closed to camping. There are over 65 miles of trails. A permit and detailed trail information can be obtained at the Visitor Center in Frijoles Canyon.

White Sands National Monument (Box 458, Alamogordo NM 88310)

This national monument occupies just a small part of the Tularosa Basin of south-central New Mexico. It is a land of alkali flats, gypsum desert and drifting dunes. There are no developed campsites in the Monument and only one primitive campsite available. Because of the continuing program of missile development at the nearby White Sands Missile Range, all overnight use must be confined to the designated area. Permission to camp is also contingent on the missile testing schedule, and because the schedule is changeable, no reservations are taken and use is on a first-come, first-served basis. Stop at the Visitors Center to register and obtain directions to the area.

Chaco Culture National Historical Park (Box 6500, Bloomfield NM 87413)

This Park, established to preserve the remains of the Pueblo Indian agricultural society of centuries ago, contains 12 large and more than 400 smaller ruins in an area about eight miles long and two miles wide. A campground in Chaco is available for overnight camping, but overnight backpacking trips are not permitted in the Park.

Gila Wilderness

This section of the Gila National Forest is part of the Mogollon Plateau, its land sharply cut by steep, rugged canyons through which flow numerous streams and rivers. Climatic conditions are diverse during each season due to the wide range of elevations. A permit is required and can be obtained by writing the Gila National Forest headquarters or in person at a Ranger Station in any of the following towns: Magdalena, Truth or Consequences, Glenwood, Mimbres, Reserve or Silver City.

Pecos Wilderness

This area lies at the southern end of the majestic Sangre de Cristo Mountains, at the headwaters of the Pecos River. Its 222,000 acres include some of the most scenic country in New Mexico, and Truchas Peak, second highest in the state, harbors many rare species of plants and animals. For a permit, write either Carson or Santa Fe National Forest, or go to a ranger station in any of these locations: Penasco, Espanola, Las Vegas, Pecos or Santa Fe.

San Pedro Parks Wilderness

These 41,132 acres of Santa Fe National Forest are located on a high, moist plateau of rolling mountaintops, with alternating areas of dense spruce and open mountain meadows. Deer, bear, turkey, grouse and elk are quite common here. For a backcountry permit, write Santa Fe National Forest or go to a Ranger District office in Cuba, Coyote or Jemez Springs.

Wheeler Peak Wilderness

The focal point of this 19,661-acre Wilderness is Wheeler Peak, 13,161' in elevation, the highest in New Mexico. The alpine tundra that covers Wheeler and other nearby peaks is rare in the Southwest. For more information, write Carson National Forest or go to the Ranger District office in Questa or Taos.

White Mountain Wilderness

Rising from the surrounding desert, the White Mountains reach to over 12,000' just outside the Wilderness. Five life zones ranging from desert to subalpine are encountered here, and the transition through life zones is one of the most rapid and abrupt found in any wilderness. Write Lincoln National Forest for more information.

Sandia Mountain Wilderness

This area of 37,232 acres covers a large portion of the Sandia Mountains immediately adjacent to the City of Albuquerque. Elevations range from 6,500 feet to well over 10,000 feet. It is easily accessible by aerial tram and nearby roads and there is an extensive trail system throughout the area. No permit is required. For current weather and trail conditions contact the Cibola National Forest headquarters.

Manzano Mountain Wilderness

This 36,402-acre wilderness covers most of the crest area of the Manzano Mountains. Upper elevations exceed 9,500 feet. There are spectacular views of the Rio Grande River valley from the Crest Trail. No permit is required. For current weather and trail conditions contact the Cibola National Forest headquarters.

Withington Wilderness

This 19,075-acre Wilderness is located in the San Mateo Mountains. This rugged Wilderness is predominantly covered by ponderosa pine and other conifer species. Visitor use is very light. No permit is required. For current weather and trail conditions contact the Cibola National Forest headquarters.

Apache Kid Wilderness

Covering 44,530 acres, this high, rugged Wilderness provides the visitor an outstanding opportunity to enjoy a high degree of solitude. A vast trail system provides access to all portions of the wilderness. Sightings of black bear, deer, elk, turkey and mountain lion are not uncommon. No permit is required. For current weather and trail conditions contact the Cibola National Forest headquarters.

Dome Wilderness

These 5,200 acres encompass a series of mesas and deep canyons, with elevations ranging from approximately 7,000 to 9,000 feet. No permit is required. Contact the Santa Fe National Forest headquarters for details.

Cruces Basin Wilderness

These 18,000 acres encompass relatively gentle terrain of mixed conifer stands and open mountain grasslands. Water is available year-round. There are no designated trails, but a number of primitive roads in the area exist. No permits are required. Contact the Carson National Forest headquarters for more information.

Latir Peak Wilderness

This 20,000-acre Wilderness is on steep, rugged land, with several mountain peaks reaching over 12,000'. (Elevations begin at around 8,000'.) There is plenty of water, and 5 trails lead into the Wilderness from the outside. No permit is required, but contact the Carson National Forest for more details.

Aldo Leopold Wilderness

These 211,300 acres are rugged, high mountains being interspersed with deep canyons. There are many trails in this area, and a permit is required. Contact the Forest Supervisor of Gila National Forest.

Capitan Mountains Wilderness

This Wilderness is 34,513 acres of very rough terrain, encompassing mostly slopes of an isolated east-west mountain range. There is a system of trails in existence, and no permit is required. Contact the Lincoln National Forest headquarters for details.

Black Range Primitive Area

This 169,356-acre Primitive Area in Gila National Forest was created to preserve the wild characteristics and resources of the rugged Black Range of mountains. The rough, rocky canyons and peaks offer solitude and relief from high desert temperatures, and it is said the famous Apache Chief Geronimo used the Black Range as a hideout. A backcountry permit is required and can be obtained by writing Gila National Forest or by going to any of the Gila Wilderness ranger stations (see "Gila Wilderness").

Blue Range Primitive Area
About 36,000 acres of this Primitive Area, which lies at the southern edge of the Colorado Plateau, are located in the New Mexico section of the Apache National Forest. (For details see the Arizona section.)

National Forests

Carson National Forest
Forest Service Bldg.
Box 558
Taos NM 87571
(505) 758-2238

Cibola National Forest
10308 Candelaria NE
Albuquerque NM 87112
(505) 766-2185

Gila National Forest
2610 North Silver Street
Silver City NM 88061
(505) 388-1986

Santa Fe National Forest
Box 1689
Santa Fe NM 87501
(505) 988-6970

Lincoln National Forest
Federal Bldg.
11th and New York
Alamogordo NM 88310
(505) 437-6030

Arizona

Grand Canyon National Park (Box 129, Grand Canyon AZ 86023)
This Park, focusing on the world-famous Grand Canyon of the Colorado River, encompasses the entire course of the river and adjacent uplands from the southern boundary of Glen Canyon National Recreation Area to the eastern boundary of Lake Mead National Recreation Area. The forces of erosion have exposed an immense variety of formations which illustrate vast periods of geological history. Besides providing insights into geologic history, the Grand Canyon is a vast biological museum. The "grand" canyon and its unnumerable side canyons are bounded by high plateaus that have cool north-facing slopes and hot south-facing slopes, year-round and intermittent streams, and seasonal climatic variations. Life is abundant here—from desert life forms at the lower elevations near the river to the conifer forest communities on the rims.

Because the canyon is such a fragile environment, there are more than the usual number of regulations and restrictions governing its overnight use. Permits are required for overnight camping beneath the rim, with a time limit of 7 nights per hike in popular areas. Advance reservations are necessary and are accepted three months in advance of the month requested. For example, reservations for any day in July will be accepted beginning April 1. Requests received more than three months in advance will be returned. Spring time is the most popular time of year to hike the canyon, since most schools are on break and the weather is usually good then. (Summer temperatures consistently exceed 100°F and make hiking difficult and unpleasant.) Available space is filled on a first-come, first-served basis. Reservation requests must specify the number of people in your party, campgrounds and trails desired, and dates proposed for each. To make reservations, write or call the Backcountry Reservation Office, Grand Canyon National Park AZ 86023. (602) 638-2474. This office does not make reservations for campground space on the rim, river trips, mule trips, lodging, or trips into the Havasupai Indian Reservation.

NOTE: The Park will be changing its reservation system in 1983 to improve its efficiency and equity. So check first with the Reservation Office before making plans.

For information on South Rim (open year-round) lodging, contact Grand Canyon National Park Lodges, Grand Canyon AZ 86023, (602) 638-2401. The National Park Service also maintains several campgrounds on the South Rim.

The 320 campsites at the Mather Campground on the South Rim can be reserved in advance by going in person to any one of California's 150 Ticketron outlets, or by mail from throughout the US by writing the Ticketron Reservation Office, Box 2715, San Francisco CA 94126. Ticketron will not accept telephone reservations. Reservations may be made up to eight weeks in advance, starting March 30 for the period between Memorial Day and Labor Day. Mail orders must be received in Ticketron's San Francisco office at least two weeks in advance so that they can be processed and the reservation ticket returned. Reservations also may be made in person through a computer terminal at the Park. Campsites at the other campgrounds on the South Rim and North Rim will remain on a first-come, first-served basis.

To make reservations for lodging at the North Rim (which, due to heavy snowfall, is closed from mid-October to mid-May) write or call TWA Services, 4045 South Spencer St., Las Vegas NV 89109, (800) 634-6951. Both the National Park Service and the Forest Service maintain campgrounds near the North Rim.

Petrified Forest National Park (Petrified Forest National Park AZ 86025)
The Park is the most colorful part of the Painted Desert of northern Arizona and contains the world's finest concentration of petrified wood. Traces of iron, manganese and carbon have stained the silica, giving the

sandstone, shale and clay a rainbow hue. There are few developed trails in the Park; the majority of the Park is seen by cross-country hiking. The clean air and lack of vegetation, with a variety of unique landmarks, are conducive to this type of travel. The Park is open year-round, though spring and fall are the best times to hike. Summer heat and rain and winter snows make these seasons less desirable.

There are no overnight accommodations in the Park. Motels and facilities are available in Holbrook and Winslow AZ. There are no campgrounds in the Park, but there is a public campground 50 miles southeast of the park at Lyman Lake State Park. Two private campgrounds, Red Arrow in Joseph City and KOA Campground in East Holbrook, provide camping facilities.

A backcountry permit is required for all overnight stays. It may be obtained from a ranger at either of the Visitor Centers or entrance stations. Hiking is permitted anywhere in the Park; backpacking is permitted only in two wilderness areas of the Park.

Navajo National Monument (Tonalea AZ 86044, [602] 672-2366)
The Monument preserves the cliff dwellings of the Anasazi Indian farmers who lived in this canyon country of northeastern Arizona seven centuries ago. The three great dwellings, Betatakin, Keet Seel and Inscription House, that make up the Navajo National Monument mark the culmination of Anasazi culture in the Kayenta area.

Permits are required for the overnight backpack to the primitive camp at Keet Seel. They may be obtained at the Betatakin Visitor Center. To visit the Keet Seel ruin, you may make reservations up to 60 days in advance. Visitation is limited to 20 persons per day. The 30 campsites at Headquarters are open from mid-May through October on a first-come, first-served basis.

Saguaro National Monument (Route 8, Box 695, Tucson AZ 85731)
The Monument is located near Tucson and is made up of two units. The Rincon Mountain Unit is 16 miles east of Tucson; the Tucson Mountain Unit is 15 miles west of Tucson. The Monument was established primarily to protect the superb stands of the giant saguaro cactus that grow in these two picturesque sections of the Sonoran Desert. Backpacking is possible year-round.

There are no overnight rental accommodations or campgrounds in the Monument. Motels and restaurants can be found in Tucson.

A permit is required to camp overnight in the 63,360-acre backcountry of the Rincon Mountain Unit. Permits are available at the Visitor Center.

Organ Pipe Cactus National Monument (Route 1, Box 100, Ajo AZ 85321)
The 330,690-acre park was established to preserve desert plants, animals

and natural features in a segment of the Sonoran Desert landscape, which stretches from northwestern Mexico to southeastern California. Stark mountains, rocky canyons, creosotebush flats, and dry washes typify this beautiful land. The open nature of the desert vegetation makes it ideal for cross-country hiking, which is possible almost anywhere in the Monument. Winter days are sunny and warm. Clear skies and progressively hotter days arrive during April, May and June. Temperatures of 95° to 110° are common in summer.

Backcountry permits, required for overnight stays, may be obtained at the Visitor Center or by mail.

Glen Canyon Dam and National Recreation Area (Box 1507, Page AZ 86040)

Although the mailing address for this area is Page, Arizona, most of the recreation area is in Utah. Please refer to our Utah listing for complete information.

Bureau of Land Management (2400 Valley Bank Center, Phoenix AZ 85073)

All 12½ million acres of land administered by the Bureau of Land Management in Arizona are open to backpacking. However, there are three BLM Primitive Areas that offer outstanding backpacking opportunities:

Paria Canyon Primitive Area This 40-mile-long river canyon starts in Utah and ends at Lee's Ferry on the Colorado River in the Glen Canyon National Recreation Area. For permits and additional information write: BLM, 320 North 1st East, Kanab UT 84741, (801) 644-2962.

Pauite Primitive Area About 55 square miles of wild, rugged land make up this primitive area in the extreme northwest part of Arizona, near the Utah and Nevada borders. Included in the area are 35,092 acres of the Virgin Mountains. The natural diversity and wild character of these mountains combine to make an area that is highly appealing to hikers. There are no trails in this Primitive Area. Write BLM, Arizona Strip District, Box 250, St. George UT 84770, (801) 673-3545.

Aravaipa Canyon Primitive Area Aravaipa is a 7½-mile-long canyon through which the waters of Aravaipa Creek flow year-round. The 4,044 acres of land that form this area are home to a fascinating variety of desert plants and animals. Spring and fall are ideal times to hike; summer temperatures can rise to over 100 in this low-desert elevation. Permits and a small fee are required, and since use is limited to 50 persons per day, advance reservations are necessary during the spring and fall months and for all weekend visits. Write: BLM, 425 East 4th St., Safford AZ 85546, (602) 428-4040.

Blue Range Primitive Area

Lying at the southern edge of the Colorado Plateau, in Apache National Forest, the Blue Range is rugged and beautiful, with many geologic and scenic attractions. The Mogollon Rim forms the northern boundary.

Elevations range from 4500' to 9100'. There is mixed conifer and ponderosa pine in the higher elevations, pinyon-juniper and scrub in the
lower elevations. The area is traversed by many miles of trail; water is
often scarce.

Chiricahua Wilderness

Jutting from the floor of the desert are the rugged pine-clad peaks of
the Chiricahua Mountains. Variations in elevation, exposure, slope and
moisture permit a wide variety of plant and animal life. The 18,000
acres of this Wilderness Area are located in the Coronado National
Forest in the southeast corner of Arizona near the New Mexico border.
No permits are needed to use this area. For further information write
Coronado National Forest.

Galiuro Wilderness

The Galiuro Range is a very rough, brushy desert mountain range,
rising abruptly from the desert floor. The flanks form a series of spectacular cliffs and benches. Travel is extremely difficult due to the steep
topography and dense brush. Water is scarce and high temperatures
discourage travel during the summer months. No permits are needed.
For further information write the Coronado National Forest.

Mazatzal Wilderness

This wilderness in Tonto National Forest embraces the north end of the
Mazatzal Range. These are predominately desert mountains, exceeding-
ly rough and precipitous. Elevations range from 2,500' to 7,888'. There
are about 180 miles of trails; their condition varies from excellent to
poor. Hikers should be prepared for difficult travel conditions and
should carry water. No permits are required. Write Tonto National
Forest for further information.

Mount Baldy Wilderness

Mount Baldy is an extinct volcano in Apache National Forest which has
experienced three distinct periods of glaciation. The topography varies
from gently sloping timbered benches to extremely steep, rock-strewn
mountainsides, cut by deep canyons. This is the only wilderness area in
Arizona that contains the subalpine vegetation zone. The summit of Mt.
Baldy and the last half mile of trail to the top are on the Ft. Apache
Indian Reservation. Persons using that area must have a permit, available for a fee from Tribal headquarters, Box 218, White River AZ
85941. Permits must be picked up in person. No other permits are required to use the area. For further information write Apache National
Forest.

Pine Mountain Wilderness

The 20,062 acres of this area are located in both Prescott and Tonto
National Forests. Lying along the high Verde Rim, the area stands as an
island of tall, green timber, surrounded by desert mountains with hot,
dry mesas and deep canyons. The elevation ranges from 4,600' to 6,800'

atop Pine Mountain. For more information write Prescott National Forest.

Pusch Ridge Wilderness

This is a new Wilderness Area, designated as such in 1978. The 56,430 acres of Pusch Ridge are in the Santa Catalina Mountains, which make up the northeastern boundary of the city of Tucson. This is a steep, rugged area cut by canyons. The elevation ranges from about 2,500' to 9,157'. There are about 100 miles of trails; no permits are required. At the present time there is little published information available on the area. If you have specific questions write Coronado National Forest.

Sierra Ancha Wilderness

Sierra Ancha is located in Tonto National Forest. The 20,850-acre area is exceptionally rough, scenic and inaccessible. The desert mountains include precipitous box canyons, high vertical cliffs and dense chaparral fields. The extremely rough topography limits, and in some places prohibits, cross-country travel. The elevation varies from 4,000' to 7,400'. No permits are required. Write Tonto National Forest for further information.

Superstition Wilderness

Located in Tonto National Forest, this 124,140-acre area contains some exceptionally rugged canyons and mountains. Its winding watercourses and "look-alike" country can be confusing to the unknowledgeable visitor. Other areas of this Wilderness contain more rolling terrain and are more conducive to cross-country travel. There are about 140 miles of trails within the area. Elevations range from 2,000' to 6,265' at Mound Mountain. Write Tonto National Forest for further information.

Sycamore Canyon Wilderness

The 47,762 acres of this Wilderness are located in Coconino, Kaibab and Prescott National Forests. This area contains a unique canyonland environment. The canyon cuts through the Colorado Plateau at its southern edge and through the Mogollon Rim, and winds 20 miles along Sycamore Creek, spreading as much as seven miles from rim to rim. No permits are required. Write to any of the three National Forests mentioned above for further information.

National Forests

Apache National Forest
Sitgreaves National Forest
Box 640
Springerville AZ 85938
(602) 333-4301
Coconino National Forest
2323 Greenlaw Lane
Flagstaff AZ 86011
(602) 779-3311

Prescott National Forest
344 South Cortez St.
Prescott AZ 86301
(602) 445-1762
Tonto National Forest
Box 13705
102 S. 28th St.
Phoenix AZ 85002
(602) 261-3205

Coronado National Forest
Federal Building
301 West Congress
Tucson AZ 85701
(602) 792-6483

Kaibab National Forest
800 S. 6th Street
Williams AZ 86046
(602) 635-2681

MOUNTAIN

Idaho, Montana, Wyoming, Colorado, Utah, Nevada

Idaho

Yellowstone National Park (Box 168, Yellowstone National Park WY 82190)
See our Wyoming listing for a description of this park.

Craters of the Moon National Monument (Arco ID 83213)
South-central Idaho has one of the most astonishing landscapes in America. Vast lava fields are studded with cinder cones whose large central depressions resemble the craters on the moon. Eighty-three square miles of the extraordinary volcanic region have been established as Craters of the Moon National Monument. Perhaps the best part of the Monument is that which lies beyond the end of the road: Craters of the Moon Wilderness Area. This 68-square-mile area offers hikers a unique wilderness experience among the weird yet beautiful volcanic formations. Only three trails penetrate this Wilderness, and then only for a short distance. After that, travel is cross-country.

A campground is located a short distance from the Park entrance; it is open from May to September. The campground will be closed for repairs for a few weeks during the summer of 1983. Campsites cannot be reserved. A backcountry permit, obtainable at the Visitor Center, is needed if you intend to stay overnight in the wilderness area.

Gospel Hump Wilderness
This 206,000-acre wilderness is located in the Nezperce National Forest about 15 miles southeast of Grangeville, Idaho. It is an area of deep canyons and high peaks. There are over 600 miles of trail in the area. Contact Nezperce National Forest for additional information.

Hells Canyon Wilderness
See our Oregon listing for a description of this area.

River of No Return Wilderness

This vast, 2,239,933-acre area occupies parts of the Payette, Bitterroot, Nezperce, Boise, Challis and Salmon National Forests. It is now the largest wilderness in the Continental U.S. Lakes dot the terrain, most of them hidden in the maze of peaks and timbered wilderness that stretches as far as the eye can see. The area also contains 216,870 acres of rugged river breaks extending more than 40 miles through an essentially unroaded area along the north side of the Salmon River. The elevation range of the area is from 2,300' to 10,052'. The area can be reached on foot, on horseback, by boat and by plane. There are about 50 outfitters providing horses, accommodations, boats, guides and air travel in the River of No Return Wilderness. Write any one of the six National Forests for complete details in planning your trip.

Sawtooth Wilderness

This 216,383-acre wilderness is located in the Sawtooth, Boise and Challis National Forests in central Idaho. This rugged area contains steep peaks, deep gorges, glacial basins, waterfalls, timbered slopes and grassy meadows. The wilderness includes the headwaters of the North Fork and the Middle Fork of the Boise River, the South Fork of the Payette River and portions of the Salmon River. Elevations vary from 5,500' to 10,751' atop Thompson Peak. There are many peaks over 10,000' in elevation. About 300 lakes dot the terrain, many of them reachable only on foot. Over 300 miles of maintained trails await the hiker; the best time for backpacking is July and August. Trout fishing is good and hunting is allowed. Permits are required for groups of 10 or more and for all stock use regardless of number. Permits may be obtained in person and by mail. Write the Sawtooth National Recreation Area Headquarters, Ketchum ID 83340, for permits and additional information.

Selway-Bitterroot Wilderness

This 1,340,681-acre wilderness lies on both sides of the Bitterroot Range, which forms part of the boundary between Idaho and Montana. It includes large parts of the Lochsa and Selway River drainages in Idaho and the Bitterroot River in Montana. The 1,089,238 acres in Idaho are administered by the Bitterroot, Clearwater and Nezperce National Forests. The 251,443 acres in Montana are managed by the Bitterroot and Lolo National Forests.

It is difficult to grasp the immensity and variety of this area. Elevations range from 1,600' on the Selway River to over 10,000' in the Bitterroot Range. This provides for a variety of land forms, flora and fauna. The area is so great, and the wilderness opportunities so varied, that a year of exploration would still leave many parts unseen. No permits are required. Write any of the National Forests mentioned above for additional information.

Bureau of Land Management

The BLM conducts a multiple-use program of the range, forest, mineral, wildlife, water and recreation resources on more than 12 million acres of land in Idaho. The BLM has a total of 25 recreation sites and also publishes an Idaho Recreation Guide, 120 pages long and free for the asking. It contains 23 maps which show locations and facilities of state parks, state lands, national forests and BLM lands. Write BLM, Idaho State Office, 550 W. Fort St., Boise ID 83724.

National Forests

Challis National Forest
Challis ID 83226
(208) 879-2285

Payette National Forest
Box 1026
McCall ID 83638
(208) 634-2255

Salmon National Forest
Forest Service Bldg.
Box 729
Salmon ID 83467
(208) 756-2215

Sawtooth National Forest
1525 Addison Ave. East
Twin Falls ID 83301
(208) 733-3698

Targhee National Forest
Box 208
St. Anthony ID 83445

Clearwater National Forest
Route 1
Orofino ID 83544
(208) 476-4541

Nezperce National Forest
Route 2, Box 475
Grangeville ID 83530
(208) 983-1950

Idaho Panhandle National Forests
(Coeur d'Alene, Kaniksu, St. Joe)
1201 Ironwood Dr.
Coeur d'Alene ID 83815
(208) 765-7561

Montana

Glacier National Park (West Glacier MT 59936)

The Park is a ruggedly beautiful, 1,013,598-acre wilderness famous for its glaciers, lakes, wildflowers and wild animals. It is a land of sharp, precipitous peaks and ridges girdled by evergreen forests and wildflower meadows. There are 590 miles of trails and 60 backcountry campgrounds. Fishing is average. Climbing is possible but not encouraged due to the crumbly nature of the sedimentary rock. Horse-related backcountry camping can be done along most trails in compliance with backcountry regulations. Opening dates of trails vary with the depth of the snow pack. Most passes are open by mid-July for hikers and a week or so later for stock.

Hotels, cabins and lodges in the Park are operated by Glacier Park, Inc., (May 15 to Sept 15 write East Glacier Park, MT 59434; Sept 15 to May 15 write Box 4340, Tucson AZ 85717). Reservations are advised; deposits required. Sperry and Granite Park Chalets are open for the use of backcountry travelers from July 1 to Labor Day. They are accessible by trail only. For rates and reservations contact Belton Chalets, West Glacier MT 59936, (406) 888-5511.

Backcountry permits are required for all hikers who intend to have a fire or camp overnight. Because the backcountry of Glacier is subject to closures due to trail failures, fires, bear activity and other unforeseen natural events, backcountry permits cannot be obtained more than 24 hours before starting your trip. Be flexible; plan alternate routes, especially during July and August, when competition is keen for available space. There is a 6-day maximum length of stay for any one itinerary (this may be extended, provided there are backcountry campsites available), with not more than 3 consecutive nights at any one campground. Permits may be obtained from information stations, visitor centers or ranger stations. Permits are issued on a first-come, first-served basis. Wood fires are permitted at many backcountry campgrounds. No license is required to fish in Glacier.

Absaroka-Beartooth Wilderness

This 904,500-acre wilderness is located in the Custer and Gallatin National Forests. It contains some of Montana's most rugged mountain country. The wilderness is in south-central Montana, stretching from just north of Yellowstone National Park to 80 miles southwest of Billings. It is largely a forested, high mountain area with interspersed mountain meadows. Elevations range from 5,900' to 12,799' atop Granite Peak, Montana's highest point. No permits are required. Contact either National Forest for additional information.

Anaconda-Pintler Wilderness

This 158,516-acre wilderness is situated in three National Forests: Beaverhead, Deerlodge and Bitterroot. It is an area of rugged mountains atop the Continental Divide in southwestern Montana. There are approximately 280 miles of trails in this wilderness, with 22 entry points. About 40 miles of the proposed Continental Divide Trail will pass through the area. No permits are needed to use the area. Write to any one of the three National Forests for additional information.

Bob Marshall Wilderness

This 1,009,400-acre wilderness is near the Montana cities of Great Falls, Kalispell and Missoula. The area extends about 60 miles from north to south along the Continental Divide. The area is noted for its outstanding hunting, fishing, scenery and geology. Elevations range from 4,000' to 9,393'. The South Fork of the Flathead River is classified as part of the National Wild and Scenic Rivers System. No permits are needed but for safety's sake it is best to register with a ranger before any trip is attempted. This area is located in and administered by both Flathead and Lewis and Clark National Forests. Write to them for additional information.

Cabinet Mountains Wilderness

The 94,272 acres of this wilderness are located in both Kaniksu (see Idaho National Forests) and Kootenai National Forests in northwest Montana. The area is composed of a series of prominent peaks and surrounding timbered valleys and ridges. Elevations range from 3,000' to 8,712' atop Snowshoe Peak. No permits are needed. Write Kootenai National Forest for more information.

Gates of the Mountains Wilderness

This small, 28,562-acre wilderness is located in the Helena National Forest in central Montana. The wilderness contains picturesque limestone formations. There are about 40 miles of trails within the area. Write Helena National Forest for more information.

Great Bear Wilderness

This 286,700-acre wilderness is located in the Flathead National Forest in the Rocky Mountains, 30 miles east of Kalispell. This is a rugged, scenic area. Elevations range from 4,000 feet along the Middle Fork of the Flathead River to 8,875' atop Mt. Wright. The Middle Fork of the Flathead River is classified as part of the National Wild and Scenic Rivers System. There are almost 300 miles of trails in the area. For additional information write Flathead National Forest.

Mission Mountains Wilderness

This 73,900-acre wilderness is an area of outstanding scenic beauty. Here the visitor will find snowcapped peaks, several small glaciers, alpine lakes, meadows, and clear cold streams. The topography is rough and broken, especially in the southern part. The northern part is more timbered, and its terrain is not as steep and rugged. There are about 70 miles of trails in the Mission Mountains. No permits are required. The area is located in, and administered by, Flathead National Forest. Contact them for more information.

Scapegoat Wilderness

This 239,936-acre area is located in three National Forests: Helena, Lewis and Clark and Lolo. It is a wilderness of unusual scenic and geologic interest bisected by the Continental Divide. Massive limestone cliffs are an extension of the "Chinese Wall" in nearby Bob Marshall Wilderness. Broad expanses of alpine and subalpine country combined with steep and rocky terrain characterize the area. No permits are required. Contact any one of the National Forests listed above for additional information.

Selway-Bitterroot Wilderness

This 1,340,681-acre wilderness lies on both sides of the Bitterroot Range, which forms the boundary between Idaho and Montana. It includes large parts of the Lochsa and Selway River drainages in Idaho and the Bitterroot River in Montana. The 1,089,238 acres in Idaho are administered by Bitterroot, Clearwater and Nezperce National Forests. The 251,443 acres in Montana are managed by Bitterroot and Lolo National Forests.

It is difficult to grasp the immensity and variety of this area. Elevations range from 1,600' on the Selway River to over 10,000' in the Bitterroot Range. This provides for a variety of land forms, flora and fauna. The area is so great, and the wilderness opportunities so varied, that a year of exploration would leave many parts unseen. Write any of the National Forests mentioned above for additional information.

Welcome Creek Wilderness

Approximately 27 miles southeast of Missoula, lies the 28,135-acre Welcome Creek Wilderness. Much of it is forested with old growth stands of lodgepole pine interspersed with groves of Douglas fir and spruce. The elevations range from 4,100' in the Rock Creek basin to 7,723' on Welcome Peak. No permits are required. Write Lolo National Forest for more details.

Spanish Peaks Wilderness

This 50,616-acre wilderness is situated in the Gallatin National Forest. Hikers here will find snowclad peaks, glacial lakes, waterfalls, mountain meadows, and colorful rock formations. Elevations range from 6,000' to 11,015' on Gallatin Peak. There are 25 peaks over 10,000'; timberline is at about 9,000'. Lakes and streams contain cutthroat, rainbow, brook and grayling trout. Write Gallatin National Forest for additional information.

Rattlesnake National Recreation Area and Wilderness

This 61,000-acre area is located north of the city limits of Missoula. Approximately 33,000 acres are wilderness; the remaining area is suited for a wider variety of recreational activities. Elevations range from 3,600' to more than 8,600'. The area contains numerous lakes, streams and waterfalls. No permits are required. Write Lolo National Forest for additional information.

Bureau of Land Management

The Bureau of Land Management in Montana manages about eight million acres of public land, and it is all open to backpacking. Of particular interest to backpackers are these five areas:

Bear Trap Canyon Primitive Area. Located 25 miles west of Bozeman off Route 84 is an awesome 9-mile gorge cut through the Madison Range by the Madison River. Here nature has created canyon walls and crags that climb almost 1,500' above the water. Commercial guides are available for those interested in floating the river. The canyon can be hiked on a primitive undeveloped trail over rather rough terrain. For additional information contact the BLM, Butte District Office, 106 N. Parkmont, Box 3388, Butte MT 59701, (406) 723-6561.

Centennial Mountains Primitive Area. Located in southwestern Montana, east of Monida, these majestic mountains received their name as a result of the arrival of the first livestock in the valley on July 4, 1876. The mountains are extremely rugged with high, open ridges that descend sharply into steep, tree-covered drainages. In spring, the meadows are a profusion of color from wildflowers. Several small lakes dot the area. An excellent area for those interested in cross-country hiking. For more information contact the BLM, Butte District Office, address and phone above.

Humbug Spires Primitive Area. Located in southwestern Montana, 25 miles south of Butte, is an area of rolling hills covered with ponderosa pine and studded by hundreds of majestic white granite spires. Nine of the spires soar between 300 and 600 feet above their surroundings. This is an area for experienced climbers as rescue operations have yet to be established so climbers are on their own. For more information contact the BLM, Butte District Office, address and phone above.

Pryor Mountain Wild Horse Range. This 45,000-acre area is located just outside the west side of Big Horn Canyon National Recreation Area. One of three such ranges in the US, the Pryor Mountains are home to about 130 wild, free-roaming horses. Many deep canyons in the area offer interesting hiking as well as the chance to see a herd of wild horses. For more information contact the BLM, Billings Resource Area, 810 E. Main St., Billings MT 59101, (406) 657-6262.

Upper Missouri National Wild and Scenic River. "Float and Hike the Wild Missouri" is the most significant historic attraction in Montana. This 149-mile segment, from Fort Benton to the Fred Robinson Bridge at Highway 191, is the only major portion of the mighty Mississippi to be preserved and protected in its natural, free-flowing state. The best way to enjoy the river is to float, camp and take morning hikes from your camp. Permits are required for all floaters between the weekend before Memorial Day and the weekend after Labor Day. They are free and may be obtained from BLM River rangers at each major launch point. For more information contact the BLM, Lewistown District Office, Airport Road, Lewistown MT 59457, (406) 538-7461.

State Parks

There are no state parks in Montana that offer backpacking opportunities; however, by writing to Department of Fish, Wildlife and Parks, 1420 E. 6th Avenue, Helena MT 59620, you can obtain a brochure describing the recreational opportunities available in Montana.

National Forests

Beaverhead National Forest
Box 1258
Skihi St. & Hwy 41
Dillon MT 59725
(406) 683-2312

Bitterroot National Forest
316 N. Third St.
Hamilton MT 59840
(406) 363-3131

Custer National Forest
Box 2556
2602 First Ave. North
Billings MT 59103
(406) 657-6361

Deerlodge National Forest
Box 400
Federal Bldg.
Butte MT 59701
(406) 723-6561 ext. 2351

Flathead National Forest
Box 147
1935 Third Ave. East
Kalispell MT 59901
(406) 755-5401

Gallatin National Forest
Federal Bldg.
Box 130
Bozeman MT 59715
(406) 587-5271

Helena National Forest
Federal Building
Drawer 10014
Helena MT 59626
(406) 449-5201

Kootenai National Forest
Box AS
West Hwy 2
Libby MT 59923
(406) 293-6211

Lewis & Clark National Forest
1601 2nd Ave. North
Box 871
Great Falls MT 59403
(406) 727-0901

Lolo National Forest
Fort Missoula, Bldg. 24
Missoula MT 59801
(406) 329-3557

Wyoming

Yellowstone National Park (Box 168, Yellowstone National Park WY 82190)
This is the world's greatest geyser area, with Old Faithful and some 10,000 other thermal features. Here too are lakes, waterfalls, high mountains, and the Grand Canyon of the Yellowstone—all set apart in 1872 as the world's first national park. Yellowstone comprises more than 2,000,000 acres in Wyoming, Montana and Idaho.

There are over 1000 miles of maintained backcountry trails, and permits may be obtained in person at all ranger stations and visitor centers. Permits designate specific sites to be camped at on specific dates. Due to dense, uniform forests, hikers are advised to follow trails—hiking near backcountry thermal areas can be dangerous and destructive. Trails and campsites are subject to closure without advance notice due to bear activity or natural fires. Camping is allowed year-round, but during winter months (November 1–April 30) permittees must check in at a ranger station *after* completing a trip.

Most campgrounds are open from June through August or September, and limited camping is available all year. For information on accommodations within the park, write TWA Services, Inc., Yellowstone National Park WY 82190.

Grand Teton National Park (P.O. Drawer 170, Moose WY 83012)
The Tetons in northwest Wyoming soar more than a mile above the
sagebrush flats and morainal lakes of Jackson Hole. The Tetons are a
striking example of fault-block mountains, and few horizons are as inspiring as the massively rugged, 40 mile-long cluster of the Tetons rising
without foothills, abruptly from the plain.

There are more than 200 miles of hiking trails in the Park, and beginning elevation for most trails is about 6800 feet. Most high-country
trails are snow-covered until early July. Valley-floor trails are generally
free of snow by mid-June. A backcountry permit, required for all overnight backcountry use, may be obtained at the Moose Visitor Center
(which is open all year) or at Jenny Lake Ranger Station or Colter Bay
Visitor Center during the summer months.

Definite backcountry user capacities have been set, so advance reservations are suggested (although 30% of permits are set aside and issued on
a first-come, first-served basis). Reservations are accepted only by mail
from October 1st to June 1st of each year.

The Park contains five Park-operated campgrounds, which are available
on a first-come, first-served basis. There is also a wide selection of
lodgings within the Park, and advance reservations are recommended.
Write the Park for a listing of the names and addresses of these private
concessioners.

Bridger Wilderness

This wilderness's 392,169 acres are located in the Wind River Range,
with elevations from 9,500' to 13,804' on Gannett Peak, the highest in
Wyoming. The area is characterized by massive granite outcroppings,
and hundreds of lakes and streams dot the terrain. No permit is required. For details contact the Bridger-Teton National Forest headquarters in Jackson, or write the District Ranger, Pinedale Ranger
District, Box 220, Pinedale WY 82941.

Teton Wilderness

This 557,312-acre wilderness is a region of high plateaus, large valleys
and mountain meadows that can be easily traversed. Of special interest
is Two Ocean Pass, where Two Ocean Creek divides and sends one
stream to the Pacific and one to the Atlantic. This is summer range
country for the Jackson Hole elk herd. No permit is required. For details on backpacking, contact the Bridger-Teton National Forest in
Jackson, or write the District Ranger, Buffalo Ranger District, Box 278,
Moran WY 83013.

North Absaroka Wilderness

This 351,104-acre wilderness is located in the Shoshone National Forest
along the northeastern border of Yellowstone National Park. The land
is rough, marked by steep canyons, glaciers, and alpine lakes with

meadows and forests covering the lower slopes. Trails cover the area, with many leading into Yellowstone. Rugged terrain confines most use to valley bottoms. This area is prime habitat for the grizzly bear, and special care needs to be exercised in location of campsites, food preparation and food storage. Permits are not required. More information may be obtained by contacting Clarks Fork Ranger District, Box 1023, Powell WY 82435, (307) 754-2407, or Wapiti Ranger District, Box 2140, Cody WY 82414, (307) 527-6241.

Savage Run Wilderness

This Wilderness covers approximately 14,940 acres of forested land 40 miles west of Laramie. Elevations vary from 8,000' to 10,000'. Steep-sided canyons are located at the low elevations, while rolling, plateau-like terrain is at higher elevations. No wilderness permit is necessary. For details, write the Medicine Bow National Forest office in Laramie.

Cloud Peak Wilderness

This 136,905-acre area is named after its highest point, 13,161-foot Cloud Peak. Lowest point is the Main Fork of Paintrock Creek, at about 8,500 feet. Nearly vertical walls, 1,000 to 5,000 feet high, form an impressive backdrop to the surrounding area; the granite west side of Cloud Peak is dramatic in its gray solidity. The Cloud Peak area contains 256 fishing lakes and 49 miles of fishing streams, and resident wildlife includes elk, moose, deer, mountain sheep, bear, fox, and coyote. No permit is required. Write Bighorn National Forest for more information.

Fitzpatrick Wilderness

This 191,103-acre area in the Shoshone National Forest shares a long stretch of the Continental Divide with the Bridger Wilderness. It contains the highest peak in Wyoming; the Gannett Peak at 13,785'. Much of the area is bare granite, shaped by past glacial action. There are still live glaciers scouring the rock. Several rugged trails climb up above timberline through deep canyons. Access to the wilderness is very poor, being limited on the east side to the Trail Lake Ranch road and Glacier Trail, near the base of Gannett Peak. Access along the eastern boundary through the Wind River Indian Reservation is not generally permitted. Permits are not required. For more information contact the Lander Ranger District, Box FF, Lander WY 82520, (307) 332-5460 or Wind River Ranger District, Box 186, Dubois WY 82513. (307) 455-2466.

Popo Agie Wilderness (Proposed)

This 81,820-acre area located in the Shoshone National Forest on the east side of the Wind River Range shares the Continental Divide with the Bridger Wilderness which is on the west side. It is an area born of glacial action, with barren, windswept crags, alpine meadows and over 200 lakes. These southern slopes of the Wind River Range offer seven major trails with fine backpacking opportunities, including tie-ins with Bridger Wilderness trails. This high country is seldom open before mid-

July, and snowstorms can be expected above timberline at any time of
the year. Permits are not required. For more information contact the
Lander Ranger District, Box FF, Lander WY 82520, (307) 332-5460.

Washakie Wilderness

This 687,132-acre wilderness was created by combining the former
South Absaroka Wilderness with the Stratified Primitive Area. The
wilderness is located in the Shoshone National Forest. It borders Yellowstone National Park on the southeast in the southern Absaroka
Mountains. The area is volcanic in origin with sparse forests and rocky
crags. Many miles of trails take the visitor among the mountains and
valleys of this wilderness. Heaviest use occurs along valley bottoms.
This is prime grizzly country, and special precautions should be taken
with food and campsites. No permits are required. For more information contact the Wind River Ranger District, Box 186, Dubois WY
82513, (307) 455-2466 or Greybull Ranger District, Box 158, Mee-
teetse WY 82433, (307) 868-2379 or the Shoshone National Forest
Headquarters in Cody WY.

National Forests

Bridger-Teton National Forests
Forest Service Building
Box 1888
Jackson WY 83001
(307) 733-2752

Bighorn National Forest
1969 S. Sheridan Ave.
Sheridan WY 82801
(307) 672-0751

Medicine Bow National Forest
605 Skyline Dr.
Laramie WY 82070
(307) 745-8971

Shoshone National Forest
Box 2140
West Yellowstone Hwy.
Cody WY 82414
(307) 527-6241

Colorado

Rocky Mountain National Park (Estes Park CO 80517)

Embracing some of the highest altitudes within the National Park System, this 266,943-acre Park is a climber's and hiker's paradise. There
are more than 300 miles of trails, providing easy access to remote sections of the Park. The Arapaho National Recreation Area is adjacent to
the Park and can be reached by road or trail. There are few privately
owned overnight accommodations in the Park. For information on
facilities adjacent to the Park, write to the Chamber of Commerce at
either Estes Park CO 80517 or Grand Lake CO 80447. The Park has
five roadside campgrounds available on a first-come, first-served basis.
Two are open year-round, one on the eastside and one on the westside.

Backcountry permits, available either at Park Headquarters or by mail,
are required for all overnight stays and technical climbs in the Park. Per-

mits may be obtained in advance or upon arrival; however, the number issued is limited. To obtain permits campers must know the names of the campsite(s) where they wish to spend each night. Permits are good only at the location and date on the permit. By writing or calling the Backcountry Office, Rocky Mountain National Park, Estes CO 80517, (303) 586-2371, you can obtain the necessary information required to obtain permits by mail. Phone calls concerning reservation requests and changes are not accepted during June, July, August and September.

Colorado National Monument (Fruita CO 81521)

This 20,445-acre area in west-central Colorado is characterized by red-rock canyons lined with sheer cliffs, broad, tree-covered mesas, towering monoliths and intriguing rock formations. There are now 21 miles of constructed trails in the backcountry plus numerous other routes that have not been officially designated or improved. A complete lack of drinking water in the backcountry is the greatest deterrent to extended stays. Spring and fall are the best seasons for hiking. A campground near the Visitor Center is available on a first-come, first-served basis. Backcountry camping is permitted in any location lying more than ¼ mile from constructed roads and 50 yards from designated trails. Backcountry users are not strictly required to register in advance, but for their own safety it is advised.

Dinosaur National Monument (Dinosaur CO 81610)

The monument takes its name from a remarkable deposit of fossil bones in the southwest corner of the area. The Green and Yampa rivers flow through this rugged canyon wilderness, providing pleasant stream-side habitats. There are just a few miles of trails in the Park, but cross-country travel is possible. The monument has no overnight facilities. There are two developed campgrounds as well as several backcountry campgrounds. All use is on a first-come, first-served basis.

A permit, obtainable at either Visitor Center, is required for overnight stays in the backcountry.

Great Sand Dunes National Monument (Mosca CO 81146)

This 38,951-acre Monument is located at the base of the Sangre de Cristo Mountain Range. Here you will find huge sand dunes, some over 600' high, that were created when sand, blown from the southwest, was trapped by the mountains.

Camping is year-round within the monument, available on a first-come, first-served basis. There are four designated backcountry sites, two accessible by 4-wheel drive and two which are strictly backpacking sites. Trailheads leading to the Sangre de Cristo Mountains in Rio Grande National Forest begin within the Monument. Backcountry camping is allowed, by permit, in most of the wilderness area of the park. A permit is also required for backcountry campers using the Monument as a point of origin. Permits are available at the Visitor Center.

Big Blue Wilderness

This 97,700-acre area is located in the Uncompahgre National Forest. It is an area of high, jagged, rocky peaks and flat alpine ridges bisected by deep, precipitous canyons. There are approximately 80 miles of trails in the wilderness, which also contains Uncompahgre Peak at 14,309' and Weterhorn Peak at 14,015'. Contact Uncompahgre National Forest for more information.

Cache la Poudre Wilderness

This 9,308-acre area was designated in 1980. It lies in the ponderosa-pine/mountain shrub zone south of the Poudre Canyon in the Arapaho-Roosevelt National Forests. There are no trails or lakes and access is difficult to this rugged, dry, rocky region. No permits are required. Write the Arapaho-Roosevelt National Forests for more information.

Collegiate Peaks Wilderness

This 159,900-acre area is located in the San Isabel, Gunnison and White River National Forests. The area has rough and rugged terrain with many scenic vistas. The wilderness has a 17-mile portion of the proposed Continental Divide National Scenic Trail. Write any of the three national forests for more information.

Commanche Peak Wilderness

This 66,644-acre area, located in the Arapaho-Roosevelt National Forests, adjoins the north boundary of Rocky Mountain National Park. No permits are required. For more information contact Estes-Poudre Ranger District, 148 Remington St., Fort Collins CO 80524, (303) 482-3822.

Eagles Nest Wilderness

This 133,915-acre area is administered by White River National Forest. This is high alpine country located 70 miles east of Denver and just north of Vail. No permits are required. For information on where to hike, campsites, trails, etc. contact the District Ranger, 101 West Main, Drawer Q, Frisco CO 80443, (303) 945-5404.

Flat Tops Wilderness

This 235,230-acre wilderness is located in the Routt and White River National Forests, atop the White River Plateau. About 160 miles of trail cross this Wilderness of wide canyons, gently rolling grasslands and forests of spruce and alpine fir. There are more than 30 lakes and 100 miles of streams offering good-to-excellent fishing. No permits are required. Contact either National Forest for more complete information or Blanco Ranger District, Box 358, Meeker CO 81641, (303) 878-4039.

Holy Cross Wilderness

This 116,500-acre wilderness is located 20 miles southeast of Eagle in the San Isabel and White River National Forests. Elevations within the wilderness range from 8,000' to over 13,000'. Over 100 miles of con-

structed trails are available for both foot and horse travel through sometimes rugged terrain. No permits are required. Write either national forest for more information.

Hunter Fryingpan Wilderness

This 74,450-acre wilderness is located just east of Aspen in White River
National Forest. No permits are required. For the most complete infor-
mation obtainable contact the Aspen Ranger District, 806 W. Hallam
St., Aspen CO 81611, (303) 925-3445.

Indian Peaks Wilderness

This 73,391-acre wilderness is located in the Arapaho-Roosevelt National Forests south of Rocky Mountain National Park. The portion of
the wilderness that is east of the Continental Divide receives extremely
heavy use, and open campfires are prohibited. Permits are required for
groups larger than 10 persons and/or 15 horses. Contact Sulphur Ranger
District, Star Route Highway 34 and 40, Granby CO 80446, (303) 887-
3331 or Boulder Ranger District, 2995 Baseline Road, Room 16, Boulder CO 80303, (303) 444-6001 for more detailed information.

La Garita Wilderness

Located in Gunnison and Rio Grande National Forests, this 108,486-
acre wilderness is noted for its alpine terrain astride the Continental
Divide. The area features two peaks over 14,000' in elevation. Streams
and lakes contain native cutthroat and eastern brook trout. La Garita
is accessible from July through September. No permits are required.
Write either National Forest for additional information.

Lizard Head Wilderness

This 41,158-acre area is located in San Juan and Uncompahgre National
Forests. The terrain is rugged and extremely scenic; three peaks in the
area are over 14,000' in elevation. Fifty miles of trails are available to
the hiker. The elevation range is from 9,500' to 14,250'. Hunting and
fishing are fair to good. No permits are required. Contact either National Forest for additional information.

Lost Creek

This 106,000-acre Wilderness, located in Pike National Forest, is named
for Lost Creek which disappears and reappears many times as it travels
through rugged terrain. There are about 75 miles of trail in the wilderness, which lies less than 40 miles southwest of Denver. The elevations
range from 8,000' to 12,431' at Bison Peak. No permits are required.
Write Pike National Forest for additional information.

Maroon Bells-Snowmass Wilderness

This 174,000-acre area, located in White River and Gunnison National
Forests, is one of the most picturesque natural regions in Colorado.
About five miles southwest of Aspen, it offers 130 miles of hiking
trails, a variety of climbing experiences and great fishing opportunities.

No permits are needed. Write Aspen Ranger District, 806 W. Hallam St., Aspen CO 81611, (303) 925-3445, or Gunnison National Forest for additional information.

Mt. Evans Wilderness

This 73,480-acre wilderness, designated in 1980, lies 30 miles southwest of Denver. Much of the area is above timberline. No permits are required. For more information contact Clear Creek Ranger District, 101 Chicago Creek, Box 730, Idaho Springs CO 80452, (303) 567-2901 or Pike National Forest.

Mt. Massive

The 26,000 acres of this Wilderness are located in Pike National Forest near Leadville. The area contains Colorado's second highest peak, Mt. Massive at 14,421'. Along the Continental Divide, the wilderness joins the Hunter Fryingpan Wilderness. The area is characterized by alpine mountains and ridges sloping off to spruce and lodgepole pine forests at lower elevations. High mountain lakes are numerous. No permits are required. Write Pike National Forest for more information.

Mt. Sneffels Wilderness

This 16,200-acre area is located in the Uncompahgre National Forest. It is an area of mountainous, steep terrain dominated by Mt. Sneffels at 14,150'. Write Uncompahgre National Forest for more information.

Mt. Zirkel Wilderness

Located in the Routt National Forest and named for its highest peak, 12,200' Mt. Zirkel, this 72,472-acre area is noted for its many alpine lakes. The Sawtooth Range along the Continental Divide forms the nucleus of the Mt. Zirkel Wilderness. No permits are required. Write Routt National Forest for additional information.

Neota Wilderness

This 9,924-acre area near Cameron Pass was designated in 1980. The wilderness is located in the Arapaho-Roosevelt National Forests. It contains only two miles of trails and two small lakes. No permits are required. Contact the Arapaho-Roosevelt National Forests for more information.

Never Summer Wilderness

This area, designated in 1980, contains 14,100 acres at the southern terminus of the Never Summer Range. Main access is through the Kawuneeche Valley area of Rocky Mountain National Park north of Grand Lake. No permits are required. For additional information contact the Arapaho-Roosevelt or Routt National Forests or Sulphur Ranger District, Star Route Highway 34 and 40, Granby CO 80446, (303) 887-3331.

Raggeds Wilderness

This 59,200-acre wilderness is located in the Raggeds and Ruby Mountain Ranges north of Gunnison. It is a low-use area with few lakes and approximately 45 miles of trails. The elevations range from 7,000' to 13,000'. Contact either the Gunnison or White River National Forest for more information.

Rawah Wilderness

This 73,899-acre wilderness is located along the Medicine Bow Divide north of Cameron Pass. Part of the area is extremely rugged; the elevation averages over 11,000'. It is noted for its fishing waters, though lake areas receive extremely heavy summer use. Permits are required for groups larger than 10 persons and/or 15 horses. For more information contact either Arapaho-Roosevelt National Forest or Redfeather Ranger District, 1600 North College Ave., Fort Collins CO 80524, (303) 482-3334, (303) 484-0036.

South San Juan Wilderness

Located in the Rio Grande and San Juan National Forests, this 133-463-acre wilderness is on the Continental Divide in the San Juan Mountains just north of the Colorado-New Mexico border. It has a good trail system which connects the numerous lakes in the area. Hunting and fishing are considered good. No permits are required. The area is open from July through September. Contact either National Forest for more information.

Weminuche Wilderness

This area consists of 463,224 acres located in San Juan and Rio Grande National Forests in southwest Colorado. The Continental Divide forms 80 miles of the backbone of this area of great beauty and diversity. Forty per cent of the area is barren rock, grass or water; the remaining 60% is forested. The elevation range is from 7,910' to 14,083'. The area has about 450 miles of trails. Hunting and fishing are fair to good. No permits are required. Write either National Forest for additional information.

West Elk Wilderness

Situated in Gunnison National Forest, this 176,412-acre Wilderness has numerous streams which flow to all points of the compass. Their constant rush has formed canyons with many interesting features. The area ranges in elevation from 8,000' to 12,920'. No permits are needed. Write Gunnison National Forest for more information.

Bureau of Land Management

In addition to the national park and national forest lands, Colorado has more than eight million acres of public land managed by the BLM. The BLM has 24 developed recreation sites. You may obtain additional information on available maps, developed recreational sites and permit requirements by contacting the Bureau of Land Management, 1037 20th St., Denver CO 80202, (303) 837-4481.

State Parks

Colorado has a number of state parks and recreation areas that offer backpacking opportunities. Among them are Golden Gate Canyon State Park, Steamboat Lake State Park, Colorado State Forest and Lory State Park. Two recreation areas, Eleven Mile State Recreation Area and Chatfield State Recreation Area, have trail connections to National Forests. A $2 fee is required for backcountry, primitive camping. Campers may stay a maximum of 14 consecutive days. More detailed information may be obtained by writing the Division of Parks and Recreation, 1313 Sherman, Room 618, Denver CO 80203.

National Forests

Arapaho-Roosevelt National Forests
301 S. Howes, Box 1366
Fort Collins CO 80522
(303) 482-5155

Grand Mesa-Uncompahgre
& Gunnison National Forests
2250 Highway 50
Delta CO 81416
(303) 874-7691

Pike and San Isabel National Forests
1920 Valley Drive
Pueblo CO 81008
(303) 545-8737

Rio Grande National Forest
1803 West Highway 160
Monte Vista CO 81144
(303) 852-5941

Routt National Forest
Box 1198
137 10th St.
Steamboat Springs CO 80477
(303) 879-1722

San Juan National Forest
701 Camino del Rio
Durango CO 81301
(303) 247-4874

White River National Forest
Box 948
Old Federal Bldg.
Glenwood Springs CO 81601
(303) 945-2521

Utah

Arches National Park (Moab UT 84532)

This 73,389-acre Park lies in the heart of the famed red rock country of southeastern Utah, north across the Colorado River from the Mormon pioneer town of Moab. The Park has more natural stone arches, windows, spires and pinnacles than any other part of this country. The combined action of running water, wind, rain, frost and sun have formed this sculptured topography. There are 12 miles of designated trails; there are no designated trails in the backcountry.

No food or lodging is available in the Park. Motels, restaurants, groceries and gas are available in Moab. A campground for tents and trailers is located in the Devil's Garden section of the Park.

A backcountry permit is required to camp overnight and may be obtained from a field ranger or at the Visitor Center. There is no dependable water source in the backcountry. Hikers must be prepared to carry a minimum of a gallon of water a day. per person, during the summer months, when the daytime temperatures can reach 110°. Wood collecting and ground fires are not permitted in the Park. All campers must bring their own fuel or stove.

Capitol Reef National Park (Torrey UT 84775)

The Park lies in the slickrock country of southern Utah—an area where water has cut monoliths, arches and mazes of canyons out of a sandstone-and-shale desert. The Waterpocket Fold, the Park's major feature, is an immense, 100-mile-long buckling of the earth's crust where the land has tilted skyward, exposing the multicolored rock layers. Most hiking in Capitol Reef is into the canyons or over the top of the Waterpocket Fold. The Visitor Center is 5400' above sea level; the elevation and desert environment make the area prone to temperature extremes. Spring and fall are the best times to hike; the summer months bring 90° temperatures and thunderstorms.

There are no services in the Park. Food, fuel and lodging are available in Torrey and Boulder to the west of the Park, and in Hanksville to the east. The two campgrounds in the Park are open year-round, and all sites are assigned on a first-come, first-served basis.

A backcountry permit is required for overnight trips. It may be obtained from any Park Ranger or at the Visitor Center. Most Park water is contaminated by minerals or animals; backcountry users must carry their own.

Bryce Canyon National Park (Bryce Canyon UT 84717)

The Park is in southwestern Utah, on a high section of the Colorado Plateau. Here you will find the Pink Cliffs—a 20-mile escarpment exposed on the eastern edge of the Paunsaugunt Plateau. The plateau rim and adjacent slopes are extremely active areas of erosion; the same processes that were so active in the past in forming this sculptured landscape are still active today. There are 64 miles of trails. Hiking is best during the cooler months of spring and fall, but trails may also be hiked in summer.

Bryce Canyon Lodge is open from mid-May to early October. It has lodging, a dining room and a gift shop. For reservations write T.W.A. Service, Inc., P.O. Box TWA, Cedar City UT 84720, (801) 586-7686. The Park has two campgrounds; no reservations can be made and space is limited.

A backcountry permit is required for overnight trips; it can be obtained at the Visitor Center. You are limited to 5 days total in the backcountry. There may be no water along portions of the trails in mid-to-late summer. Be prepared to carry a supply.

Canyonlands National Park (446 S. Main St., Moab UT 84532)

The park is in southeastern Utah within a deeply eroded landscape of canyons, arches, mesas, and endless rock formations. The Colorado River and the Green River join forces at the confluence before rushing through Cataract Canyon in a series of wild, white-water rapids. This 337,570-acre park is mostly backcountry, with many miles of trails, four-wheel-drive routes and wild rivers. The park is open year-round, though the best hiking seasons are spring and autumn.

Commercial jeep trips and raft trips are available, but no other commercial facilities are available within the park. The park has two campgrounds in the developed sections, available on a first-come, first-served basis. Only one of the campgrounds has a source of water, and all backcountry travelers should carry their own supply. Normal food and lodging facilities are available at Moab and Monticello, Utah, on the east side of the Park. Green River and Hanksville, Utah, are the two closest towns to the isolated west side of the park.

A backcountry permit should be obtained at one of the Park offices for any overnight backcountry trip.

Zion National Park (Springdale UT 84767)

The 146,551-acre Park is located in southern Utah near the Arizona border. It is an area of great beauty; here you will find incredibly narrow canyons, hardly more than a few feet wide and half a mile deep. Phenomenal rock formations are seen in this colorful plateau-and-canyon country. Zion Canyon, carved by the Virgin River, is a major attraction. The Park has approximately 65 miles of backcountry trails, and is open year-round. September and October are the best months for hiking; during the summer, temperatures exceed 100° and thunderstorms are common. Spring hikers would encounter muddy conditions.

Food service, lodging and tours are operated by T.W.A. Service, P.O. Box TWA, Cedar City UT 84720. Reservations can also be made by calling (801) 586-7686. Nearby communities provide year-round accommodations and facilities. The Park has two campgrounds, offering 373 campsites on a first-come, first-served basis. There is a 14-day camping limit from May 15 to September 15.

A permit, required for camping and hiking in the Park's backcountry, can be obtained at the Visitor Center. Fishing is allowed with a Utah license.

Flaming Gorge National Recreation Area (Box 157, Dutch John, UT 84023)

This recreation area is located in both Utah and Wyoming; the Utah part is within Ashley National Forest. The construction of Flaming Gorge Dam created a 66-square-mile reservoir amid the spectacular hill-and-canyon country along the Green River. The Recreation Area consists of about 200,000 acres of land surrounding the reservoir. No backcountry permits are needed.

Glen Canyon Dam and National Recreation Area (Box 1507, Page AZ 86040)

Glen Canyon Dam was built to harness the turbulent waters of the Colorado River, which in their seaward rush had carved deeply into the soft sedimentary rock. Behind the dam, Lake Powell now stretches for more than 180 miles to the northeast, its waters filling the twisted, branched shape of Glen Canyon. The area is open year-round, though the best times for hiking are spring and autumn.

There are five developed campgrounds in the area. Several private concessioners offer lodging, food, groceries, raft trips, jeep tours and houseboat rentals. For their names and addresses write the Superintendent at Box 1507, Page AZ 86040.

For their own safety backpackers are encouraged to get a permit; however, it is not mandatory.

Bureau of Land Management (136 E. South Temple, Salt Lake City UT 84111)

The BLM manages over 21 million acres of public land in Utah. Of particular interest to backpackers are these four areas:

Dark Canyon This is a huge, impressive canyon, very isolated and mostly untouched by man. The upper reaches of the canyon are wide with many large, clear openings. Lower Dark Canyon is distinguished by an abundant supply of clear, flowing water and deep, crystalline plunge pools. Contact the Bureau of Land Management, San Juan Resource Area, Box 7, Monticello UT 84535, (801) 587-2201, to obtain the required permit or additional information.

Grand Gulch Primitive Area The Anasazi once lived and flourished in Grand Gulch, and the remains of their dwellings, pottery, tools and art work can be seen there today. Permits are required. Group size is limited to 25 persons. Large parties of 15–25 and all stock-using parties are required to obtain a permit reservation. Permits can be obtained at the Kane Gulch Ranger Station, Star Route, Blanding UT 84511, or at the San Juan Resource Area Headquarters, Box 7, Monticello UT 84535, (801) 587-2201.

Paria Canyon Primitive Area This 40-mile-long river canyon starts in Utah near US Highway 50 and ends at Lee's Ferry on the Colorado River in Glen Canyon. Hiking is in very narrow canyons with near-vertical sandstone walls. Required permits and additional information may be obtained at the BLM Kanab Resource Area, 320 North 1st East, Kanab UT 84741, (801) 644-2962.

Escalante Canyon Red sandstone formations and deep scenic canyons cut by the Escalante River make excellent backcountry hiking. The upper portion of the area is on BLM administered land and the lower portion is within the Glen Canyon National Recreation Area, administered by the National Park Service. The required permit can be obtained from the BLM Escalante Resource Area Office, Escalante UT 84726, (801) 826-4368.

High Uintas Wilderness

This 236,509-acre primitive area is located in both Ashley and Wasatch National Forests, in the northeastern part of Utah near the Wyoming border. The High Uinta Mountains have outstanding wilderness qualities, and are geologically special in that they are the highest mountain range in Utah, and the most prominent east-west-trending range in the US. Elevations vary from 8,000' to 13,528' at the summit of Kings Peak. There are about 500 lakes and over 400 miles of streams for fishing. The best time to hike is from July 1 to September 10; no permits are required. The area is divided into seven sections and a different district office manages each section. For more information write to Ashley or Wasatch National Forests.

Lone Peak Wilderness

This 30,088-acre scenic area is located in Uinta and Wasatch National Forests midway between Salt Lake City and Provo. The area is approximately eight miles wide and nine miles long. Elevations range from 5,140' to 11,326' at Little Matterhorn Peak. The area is characterized by steep, rugged, mountainous terrain with numerous peaks over 10,000'. The vegetation varies dramatically, from a manzanita brush type at lower elevations to a very fragile high alpine zone at the higher elevations. Backpacking, fishing, hunting and ski touring are some of the recreational opportunities to be enjoyed here. No permits are required for backcountry camping. The best season for hiking is from July to September. For more information write Uinta or Wasatch National Forests. Their addresses are listed under the National Forest heading below.

National Forests

Ashley National Forest
437 East Main
Vernal UT 84078
(801) 789-1181

Dixie National Forest
Box 580
82 North 100 East
Cedar City UT 84720
(801) 586-2421, 2422, 2424

Fishlake National Forest
115 E. 900 N.
Richfield UT 84701
(801) 896-4491

Manti-LaSal National Forest
599 W. Price River Dr.
Price UT 84501
(801) 637-2817

Uinta National Forest
Box 1428
88 West 100 North
Provo UT 84603
(801) 377-5780

Wasatch National Forest
Cache National Forest
8226 Federal Building
125 South State St.
Salt Lake City UT 84138
(801) 524-5030

Nevada

Hiking is permitted in Nevada's state parks, but there are no designated backpacking areas and camping is at designated campsites only. For a free brochure describing Nevada's state parks or a complimentary copy of "Nevada's Trails," write: Division of State Parks, Capitol Complex, Carson City NV 89710.

The Bureau of Land Management also operates nine Recreation Sites in Nevada, which have campsites and offer limited backpacking possibilities. There is a small fee for overnight use of some of the sites, but the National Park Service's Golden Eagle Passport is accepted. For details, write Bureau of Land Management, 300 Booth Street, Room 3008, Reno NV 89509.

Jarbridge Wilderness

This 65,000-acre area of Humboldt National Forest offers a rugged and rocky terrain, with scattered stands of aspen, mountain mahogany and limber pine at the high elevations. Elevation in this Wilderness ranges from 6,500' to 10,829'. Access to the area is on low-standard dirt roads, and the most popular areas are Jarbridge Lake and Emerald Lake.

There are 125 miles of trails in the Wilderness, and trails are usually passable by June 15th. Snow storms may occur after the 1st of October. A permit is not required. For more information, contact the Jarbridge Ranger Station, Box 508, Buhl ID 83316, or the Humboldt National Forest headquarters in Elko.

National Forests

Humboldt National Forest
976 Mountain City Hwy.
Elko NV 89801

Toiyabe National Forest
111 N. Virginia St.
Reno NV 89501

PACIFIC NORTHWEST

Oregon, Washington

Oregon

Oregon, with nearly 6,800 miles of marked trails, is one of the leading states in the nation in trail mileage. Major trails include a 465.7-mile

section of the Pacific Crest Trail, the 40-mile Rogue River Trail between
Grave Creek and Illahe west of Grants Pass, the 64-mile completed sec-
tion of the Oregon Coast Trail from the Columbia River to Tillamook
Bay, the 36-mile Timberline Trail encircling Mt. Hood, and a 204-mile
network of trails in the Columbia Gorge. For general information on
Oregon's trails, particularly those maintained by the State Park system
(including the Oregon Coast Trail), contact State Parks & Recreation
Branch, 525 Trade Street SE, Salem OR 97310. For excellent maps and
guide books to trails in the various national forests, write the US Forest
Service Regional Office, Box 3623, Portland OR 97208. There is a
charge of $1.00 for most Forest Service maps. For information on the
53 miles of trails (including 24 miles of the Lower Rogue River Trail)
maintained by the Bureau of Land Management, write them at 3040
Biddle Road, Medford OR 97501. And finally, the US Fish and Wildlife
Service maintains 27 miles of trail at four National Wildlife Refuges.
More information is available from the US Fish and Wildlife Service,
500 NE Multnomah St., Suite 1692, Portland OR 97232.

Crater Lake National Park (Box 7, Crater Lake OR 97604)
This National Park encompasses 183,180 acres in southern Oregon.
Crater Lake itself is a unique, deep-blue lake that lies in the caldera of
Mount Mazama, an ancient volcanic peak that collapsed centuries ago.
The lake is encircled by multicolored lava walls reaching 500 to 2,000
feet above the lake waters.

The Park has over 100 miles of trails, and the Pacific Crest Trail runs
through it for 25 miles. Park trails are usually snowbound from October
into July. When the trails are open, the weather is normally clear, with
occasional thunderstorms. A backcountry permit is required and can be
obtained at either of the two public-information stations or at either of
the two self-registration boxes. Camping with fires is permitted in the
backcountry. Camping parties are limited to 12 persons.

A lodge and cabins are located at Rim Village. For reservations write
Crater Lake Lodge, Inc., Crater Lake OR 97604, (503) 594-2511. A
Park campground is open from about mid-June to late September, on a
first-come, first-served basis.

Diamond Peak Wilderness
This 35,440-acre area straddles the Cascade Crest in parts of both
Deschutes and Willamette National Forests. About 50 miles of trail
traverse the Wilderness, but much of the area can be reached only by
those who wish to hike cross-country with a map, compass and the
mountain as guide. Backpacking is best after August 1, when the mosquito population has usually diminished. Permits are required. They are
self-issuing and may be obtained at the trailheads. Contact either National Forest for additional information.

Eagle Cap Wilderness
This 293,735-acre Wilderness embraces the rugged grandeur of the Wallowa Mountains in northeast Oregon. A mountain called Eagle Cap is the hub from which many streams flow, and over 50 lakes are nestled at the foot of precipitous slopes or hidden in high basins. The most popular period of use is usually July and August. Early- or late-season travelers unfamiliar with the area should obtain additional information locally, particularly if they plan to travel over the high passes. You can obtain a wilderness permit at the ranger stations in Baker, Enterprise, Joseph, La Grande, Halfway, Union or Unity; or write Wallowa-Whitman National Forest.

Gearhart Mountain Wilderness
There are 16 miles of maintained trail in this 18,709-acre Wilderness, named for its most outstanding feature, Gearhart Mountain, the highest and possibly oldest of the many volcanic domes in the mountains of south-central Oregon. The 12-mile Gearhart Trail gives visitors a fine cross-section of this area's scenic features. No permits are required, but visitors are requested to use the self-registration boxes at the trailheads.

Hells Canyon Wilderness
The section of the Snake River flowing north between Oregon and Idaho is known as the Middle Snake. Included in this section is Hells Canyon, the deepest river gorge in North America—a 20-mile slot through granite and basalt from Spring Creek down to Johnson Bar that averages 6600' in depth and is flanked by 10,000' peaks of the Seven Devils range in Idaho and the Wallowa Mountains of Oregon.

Summer temperatures here can soar into the 100's, and spring and fall are recommended visitation times. Rattlesnakes are common, poison oak is abundant, and a wide variety of spiders, ticks and insects live here. Because of the elevation and the great variety of plant life, the Hells Canyon area also contains the largest assortment of wildlife species in Oregon, including elk, deer, bear, cougar, marten, eagle and mountain sheep.

The Forest Service maintains four primitive campsites on the Oregon side between the town of Oxbow and Hells Canyon Dam. They can be reached by boat or via County Road #1039 out of the town of Copperfield. County Road #1039 ends approximately three miles from the campgrounds and a trail continues on.

There are many small campsites along the river on both the Oregon and Idaho sides downstream from Hells Canyon Dam. Numerous trails crisscross the area. No permit is required for hiking. For additional information write the Wallowa-Whitman National Forest.

Kalmiopsis Wilderness
This 190,000-acre area is located in the Siskiyou National Forest. This is harsh, rugged country with a character different from that of most

wildernesses: a land of rocky, brushy, low-elevation canyons. Cross-country travel is nearly impossible because of steep terrain and heavy brush. Rattlesnakes are common and poison oak is dense throughout the area. No permits are required, though it is advisable to register with a ranger or let a friend know where you are going and when you expect to return. For more information contact Siskiyou National Forest.

Mt. Washington Wilderness

A more rugged region than this 46,116-acre Wilderness is hard to imagine. Mt. Washington, at 7,802 feet, dominates the area. Its summit is topped by a jagged pinnacle rising hundreds of feet above the mountain. This peak offers one of the most popular rock climbs in Oregon. Hunting is good throughout the area and many of the 66 lakes support fish. The Patjens Lakes in the northwest part are the most extensively used. There are less than 50 miles of maintained trails in this wilderness. Permits are required. They are self-issuing and can be obtained at the trailheads. For more information contact Deschutes or Willamette National Forest.

Strawberry Mountain Wilderness

This 33,653-acre wilderness is located in Malheur National Forest. Dominating the scenery around the head of the John Day River in Oregon is Strawberry Mountain, elevation 9,044'. Its five glacial lakes, thousands of acres of alpine and subalpine flora, and spectacular views are a welcome retreat for the hiker, sportsman and photographer. Self-issuing permits, although not required, are available at the trailheads or at the Malheur National Forest Headquarters.

Wenaha-Tucannon Wilderness

The 177,469-acre Wenaha-Tucannon Wilderness, designated in 1978, encompasses the former 111,200-acre Wenaha Backcountry Area on the crest on the northern Blue Mountains in northeastern Oregon and southeastern Washington. There are over 195 miles of trails running from stream valleys to ridgetop skylines in this area of rugged basaltic ridges and outcroppings separated by deep canyons with steep side slopes and rapid-flowing streams. This remote area provides prime habitat for Rocky Mountain elk and mule deer; use is heavy during hunting season by horsemen. Wilderness permits are required and can be obtained by mail or in person. For more information contact Umatilla National Forest or the Pomeroy Ranger District in Pomeroy, Washington, (509) 843-1891.

Mountain Lakes Wilderness

This 23,071-acre area lies in the southern part of the Winema National Forest. Its highest point is Aspen Butte, with an elevation of 8208'. A permit is required and can be obtained at each trailhead or by writing Winema National Forest.

Mt. Hood Wilderness

Easy access makes this a heavily used wilderness area, and Mt. Hood provides a stunning backdrop to camping here. Within the 47,000 acres of Mt. Hood Wilderness, elevation ranges from 1800' to the 11,235' summit of Mt. Hood. There are about 200 miles of maintained trails, including the 36-mile Timberline Trail around Mt. Hood. Permits are self-issuing and may be obtained at all trailheads leading into the Wilderness.

Mt. Jefferson Wilderness

This 63,681-acre Wilderness is dominated by 10,497' Mt. Jefferson, with its glacier-mantled slopes. Beneath Mt. Jeff lie alpine meadows, tranquil lakes, rushing streams and sweeping expanses of forest. There are more than 160 miles of trail in the Wilderness, including a 40-mile stretch of the Pacific Crest Trail. Many of these trails lead to lakes within the Wilderness. Permits are self-issuing and may be obtained at the trailheads.

Three Sisters Wilderness

This 196,708-acre Wilderness offers about 240 miles of trail, leading to mountain-climbing take-off spots, to alpine meadows and to more than 300 lakes. It is located in Willamette and Deschutes National Forests in central Oregon. Permits are required. They are self-issuing and may be obtained at the trailheads.

National Forests

Deschutes National Forest
211 N.E. Revere St.
Bend OR 97701
(503) 382-6922

Fremont National Forest
Box 551
34 North D St.
Lakeview OR 97630
(503) 947-2151

Malheur National Forest
139 N.E. Dayton St.
John Day OR 97845
(503) 575-1731

Mt. Hood National Forest
2955 N.W. Division
Gresham OR 97030
(503) 667-0511

Ochoco National Forest
Box 490
Federal Bldg.
Prineville OR 97754
(503) 447-6247

Rogue River National Forest
Box 520
333 W. 8th St.
Medford OR 97501
(503) 776-3600

Siskiyou National Forest
Box 440
200 Greenfield Rd.
Grants Pass OR 97526
(503) 479-5301

Siuslaw National Forest
Box 1148
545 S.W. 2nd
Corvallis OR 97339
(503) 757-4480

Umatilla National Forest
2517 S.W. Hailey Ave.
Pendleton OR 97801
(503) 276-3811

Umpqua National Forest
Box 1008
2900 N.W. Stewart Parkway
Roseburg OR 97470
(503) 672-6601

Wallowa-Whitman National Forests
Box 907
Federal Office Bldg.
Baker OR 97814
(503) 523-6391

Willamette National Forest
Box 10607
211 East 7th Ave.
Eugene OR 97401
(503) 687-6521

Winema National Forest
Box 1390
Post Office Bldg.
Klamath Falls OR 97601
(503) 882-7761

Washington

In addition to backpacking opportunities in the vast acreage of national parks, national forests and wilderness areas, hiking is a popular activity in most of Washington's state parks. Some of the larger parks have substantial trail systems: Mt. Spokane, Moran, Larrabee, Rockport and Beacon Rock. For details contact the Washington State Parks and Recreation Commission, 7150 Cleanwater Lane, KY-11, Olympia WA 98504.

Olympic National Park (600 East Park Ave., Port Angeles WA 98362) Olympic National Park, an expanse of wild, glacier-studded mountains, rainforests, lakes and streams, lies within the Olympic Mountains of Washington. Mt. Olympus, at 7965', is the highest peak in the Park. On the strip of coastline to the west, hikers can enjoy beaches, cliffs, tidepools and the thriving wildlife of birds, seals and other marine animals that populate this area.

There are 600 miles of trails, and the Park is open year-round, although some roads, facilities and accommodations are closed in winter. A backcountry permit is required for all overnight trail and beach camping and it also serves as a fire permit. Permits can be obtained at all ranger stations and at some self-registration trailheads. There is a daily entrance quota in effect from mid-June to Labor Day for Lake Constance and Flapjack Lakes. Permits for Flapjack Lakes will be issued at Staircase Ranger Station, and for Lake Constance at Dosewallips. Quotas for each area can be reserved by phone only through Staircase Ranger Station at (206) 877-5569.

There are many campgrounds scattered throughout the Park, all available on a first-come, first-served basis. For a complete listing of accommodations within the Park, write the Park Superintendent or call (206) 452-4501, ext. 230.

North Cascades National Park (Sedro Woolley WA 98284)

The 789 square miles of this Park preserves an outstanding portion of the North Cascades Mountain Range near the Canadian border. The Park consists of North and South Units and is adjacent to the Ross Lake and Lake Chelan National Recreation Areas. This high stretch of the Cascades intercepts some of the continent's wettest prevailing winds, and the resulting precipitation has produced a region of varied alpine scenery. The Park has hanging glaciers, ice-falls, ice caps, glacier-carved canyons, waterfalls and alpine lakes.

There are approximately 360 miles of hiking and horse trails here. Best weather for hiking occurs between mid-June and late September. Snow is off all but the higher trails by July. Summer rainstorms are common. A backcountry permit is required for all overnight camping. Permits can be obtained at the ranger stations in Stehekin, Marblemount and Hozomeen. They are also available from the US Forest Service ranger stations in Darrington, Early Winters, Twisp and Glacier, and from the National Park Service/Forest Service information station at Chelan. They are issued on a first-come, first-served basis. There are limited guest accommodations within and adjacent to the Park. For reservations, write either Diablo Lake Resort (Box 194, Rockport 98282), Ross Lake Resort (Box 194, Rockport 98282), or North Cascades Lodge (Stehekin 98852).

Mt. Rainier National Park (Tahoma Woods, Star Route, Ashford WA 98304)

Mt. Rainier, a 14,410' dormant volcano, dominates this Park. The glacier system of Rainier is the country's most extensive "single peak" glacier system outside of Alaska. In contrast to these glaciers are the subalpine forests and flower-covered meadows that encircle the peak.

There are 305 miles of hiking trails in the Park, including the 95-mile Wonderland Trail encircling Mt. Rainier. The hiking season normally extends from mid-July to mid-October. Backcountry permits are required from June 15 through September 30. They are issued on a first-come, first-served basis and may be obtained at ranger stations up to 24 hours in advance of starting a backcountry trip. Any number of parties will be permitted to camp anywhere below 5000 feet in predominantly forested areas.

There are six campgrounds in the Park, but only Sunshine Point is open year-round. They are available on a first-come, first-served basis. For information on accommodations within the Park, write or call the Mt.

Rainier Guest Services, Star Route, Ashford WA 98304, (206) 569-2275. Rainier Mountaineering, Inc. conducts guided climbs on Mt. Rainier. Contact them at 201 St. Helens, Tacoma WA 98402, (206) 627-6242.

Ross Lake National Recreation Area (Marblemount WA 98267)

Ringed by mountains, this reservoir in the Skagit River Canyon separates the north and south units of the North Cascades National Park. Total acreage of this National Recreation Area is 117,574 acres. For more information contact the National Park Service, Skagit District, Marblemount Ranger Station, in Marblemount.

Glacier Peak Wilderness

This scenic area, 35 miles long and 20 miles wide, derives its name from 10,528' Glacier Peak, fourth highest peak in Washington. This jagged mountain of volcanic origin has more than 30 sister peaks in the area which rise from 5000 to 8000 feet above the intervening valleys. Glaciers radiate in all directions from the summit of Glacier Peak, and nearly all the higher peaks and ridges here cradle ice fields.

The Pacific Crest Trail provides one of the important routes within the Wilderness. A wilderness permit can be obtained by writing Mt. Baker-Snoqualmie National Forest (for west entry) or Wenatchee National Forest (for east entry), or in person at ranger stations in Granite Falls, Darrington, Concrete, Glacier, Skykomish, Chelan, Entiat, Lake Wenatchee or Holden.

Goat Rocks Wilderness

On the east flank of the great triangle formed by the three sentinels of the Northwest—Mt. Rainier, Mt. Adams and Mt. St. Helens—lies this 82,680-acre Wilderness. Elevations range from 3000' to the 8,201' Gilbert Peak. The Wilderness derives its name from the bands of mountain goats which inhabit its rocky crags. Summit ascents of varying difficulty are available for the alpinist, and a system of trails offers vistas of flower-studded meadows, peculiar rock formations, forested valleys and distant snow-capped peaks. For a wilderness permit, write Gifford Pinchot National Forest (for west entry) or Wenatchee National Forest (for east entry), or go to a ranger station at Chelatchie, Trout Lake, Packwood, Randle, Carson or White Pass Highway.

Mount Adams Wilderness

Mt. Adams Wilderness, named for the dominant feature of its 42,411 acres, lies along the eastern edge of Gifford Pinchot National Forest and adjoins the Yakima Indian Reservation. Good mountain roads approach to within about a mile of the boundary on the south and northwest sides. Trails lead into the area to meet with the Round-the-Mountain and Pacific Crest trails. Average elevation in the Wilderness is about 5500', approximately 500' below the absolute timberline. Some of this country is particularly rugged, especially on the east face of the mountain, where Hell-roaring Creek heads among the glaciers. For a wilderness permit write Gifford Pinchot National Forest or go to a ranger station in Chelatchie, Trout Lake, Packwood, Randle or Carson.

Pasayten Wilderness

This virtually unbroken fortress of wilderness extends 40 miles west to east and 20 miles north-south. Within this vastness is found all of the variety in topography and ground cover identified with the North Cascade mountain region. Trails give access to major drainages and a segment of the Pacific Crest Trail. For a wilderness permit, write Okanogan National Forest or go to a ranger station in Marblemount, Tonasket, Twisp or Winthrop, or the Early Winters Information Station on State Highway 20 west of Winthrop.

Alpine Lakes Wilderness

This Wilderness is managed by Mt. Baker-Snoqualmie and Wenatchee National Forests. Its glacial valleys and rugged mountains harbor numerour trout-stocked lakes. More than 400 miles of trails crisscross the area, including a section of the Pacific Crest Trail, and most trails are snow-free by August 1st. No permit is required, although there are some restrictions on camping.

Wenaha-Tucannon Wilderness

See under "Oregon" listing.

National Forests

Gifford Pinchot National Forest
500 W. 12th St.
Vancouver WA 98660
(206) 696-7500

Mt. Baker-Snoqualmie National
Forests
1022 First Ave.
Seattle WA 98104
(206) 442-0171

Okanogan National Forest
Box 950
1240 2nd Ave. South
Okanogan WA 98840
(509) 422-2704

Olympic National Forest
Box 2288
Federal Bldg.
Olympia WA 98501
(206) 753-9535

Wenatchee National Forest
Box 811
301 Yakima St.
Wenatchee WA 98801
(509) 662-4335

CALIFORNIA

Lassen Volcanic National Park (Mineral CA 96063, [916] 595-4444) This Park is mostly coniferous forest, with more than 50 lakes and streams in its 106,372 acres. It is dominated by Lassen Peak, a plug-dome volcano of 10,457' at the southern end of the Cascades. Lassen Park Road winds around three sides of Lassen Peak and affords beautiful views of the volcano, examples of its destructive action, and vistas of woodlands, meadows and lakes. The Park has 150 miles of trails, including a 19-mile section of the Pacific Crest Trail. Backpacking is possible from June to September, depending on snowfall and fire danger.

Accommodations are available at the Drakesbad Guest Ranch from about mid-June to mid-September. Write Drakesbad Guest Ranch, Chester CA 96020. Off season address is California Guest Services, P.O. Box 75, Mineral CA 96063, (916) 595-3306.

A backcountry permit, required for all overnight stays, may be obtained at Park Headquarters or any ranger station. Phone or mail requests should be made two weeks in advance by contacting the Park Superintendent at the address above.

Redwood National Park (1111 Second St., Crescent City CA 95531) Once found in many parts of the world, Coast Redwoods now grow as a natural forest only in a narrow strip along the northern California Coast. This species dates back more than 30 million years; individual trees live as long as 2,000 years and grow to heights of more than 300 feet.

The Park is 46 miles long and is divided into two main parts: the redwood forest with its associated vegetation, streams and rivers, and 30 miles of coastal and marine zone with headlands, beaches, lagoons and tidepools. Also within the Park's boundaries are three California State Parks: Jedediah Smith Redwoods, Del Norte Coast Redwoods and Prairie Creek Redwoods. Six Rivers National Forest is to the east of the Park.

There are no overnight facilities in the national park, but there are campgrounds in all three of the state parks and in Six Rivers National Forest. The sites in the state parks may be reserved through Ticketron outlets, or by mail through Ticketron, Box 26430, San Francisco CA 94126. Reservation information is available by calling toll-free (800) 952-5580 (weekdays 8 A.M. to 5 P.M.), or by writing the Reservation Office, Department of Parks and Recreation, Box 2390, Sacramento CA 95811. Campsites not filled by reservations are assigned on a first-come, first-served basis.

A camping and fire permit is required if you are camping overnight. It is obtainable from a dispenser at the Redwood Creek Trailhead.

Sequoia-Kings Canyon National Parks (Three Rivers CA 93271)
Lying in the heart of the Sierra Nevada in east-central California, Sequoia and Kings Canyon National Parks encompass more than 1,300 square miles of granite mountains, deep canyons, magnificent forests, lush meadows, clear lakes and tumbling waterfalls. From west to east, the two parks extend from the foothills near the San Joaquin Valley to the crest of the High Sierra. From north to south they stretch about 65 miles. Though separately established, they are virtually a single unit and are administered as such.

Over 700 miles of trail await the backpacker as well as many opportunities for cross-country travel. Elevations of the Sierra Crest range from about 11,000' to 14,495' atop Mt. Whitney.

Reservations for lodges and cabins should be made by contacting the Reservations Manager, Sequoia and Kings Canyon Hospitality Service, Sequoia National Park CA 93262, (209) 565-3373, or by writing Wilsonia Lodge, Kings Canyon National Park CA 93633.

The campgrounds of the two Parks have over 1,300 campsites operated by the National Park Service. Advance reservations are accepted for the 250 campsites at Lodgepole Campground in Sequoia National Park. Reservations can be made in person at any one of California's 150 Ticketron outlets, or by mail from throughout the US by writing the Ticketron Reservation Office, Box 2715, San Francisco CA 94126. Ticketron will not accept telephone reservations. Reservations may be made up to 8 weeks in advance, starting March 30, for the period between Memorial Day and Labor Day. Mail orders must be received in Ticketron's San Francisco office at least two weeks in advance so that they can be processed and the reservation ticket returned. Reservations also may be made through a computer terminal at the Park during the summer season. Campsites at the other campgrounds in the two parks will remain on a first-come, first-served basis.

Backcountry permits are required and there is a quota system. Reservations for permits for the west side are accepted beginning Feb. 1 for any period in the summer. There will be 50% of the daily quota available by reservation and 50% available on a first-come, first-served basis. Hikers calling or writing for reservations should have a trip itinerary which includes the day and place of entry, each night's camping location, the number of people in the group, the number of stock, and the day and trailhead where the trip will end.

By writing to the Chief Ranger's Office, Sequoia and Kings Canyon National Parks, Three Rivers CA 93271, you can obtain an application for a permit. Listed on the application are the daily entry quotas for all trailheads for Park trails. To phone for reservations, call (209) 565-3306.

Yosemite National Park (Yosemite National Park CA 95389)
The Park is a scenic wonderland of sculptured peaks and domes, water-

falls tumbling down granite cliffs, groves of giant sequoias and forests of pine, fir and oak, wildflowers in alpine meadows, hundreds of species of birds and mammals, and scenic drives and trails to areas of high-country grandeur.

The Park offers many types of activities: bike and horse rentals, swimming, fishing, rock climbing, camping, and of course the opportunity to hike the Park's 768 miles of trails.

There are all types of lodging available, from tent camping to the luxurious Ahwahnee Hotel. Reservations—strongly recommended at all times—can be made through the Yosemite Park and Curry Company, Yosemite National Park CA 95389, (209) 373-4171. They will also take reservations for the six High Sierra Camps, which are generally in operation from early July through Labor Day. It is possible to hike the High Sierra loop, one of the most scenic trips in the Sierra Nevada, and visit all the camps: Glen Aulin, May Lake, Sunrise, Merced Lake, Vogelsang and Tuolumne Meadows.

Auto campgrounds are located in the Park's developed areas. The sites at five campgrounds in the valley may be reserved in advance. Reservations may be made up to eight weeks in advance, starting March 30, for the period between Memorial Day and Labor Day. Campsites can be reserved in advance by going in person to any one of California's 150 Ticketron outlets, or by mail from throughout the US by writing the Ticketron Reservation Office, Box 2715, San Francisco CA 94126. Ticketron will not accept telephone reservations. Mail orders must be received in Ticketron's San Francisco office at least two weeks in advance so that they can be processed and the reservation ticket returned. Reservations also may be made in person through a computer terminal at the Park. Any campsites that are not reserved will be available on a first-come, first-served basis as will the two walk-in campgrounds in the valley.

Wilderness permits are required for all overnight stays in the Park's back-country. From February 1 to May 31 write the Backcountry Office, Box 577, Yosemite National Park CA 95389, to reserve a permit. If you know when you will be hiking during the summer, this is the way to go, since 50% of the daily trailhead quota for each backcountry area is available for reservation. The remaining 50% is set aside on a first-come, first-served basis, and you can get one of these permits up to 24 hours before actual trailhead departure.

Channel Islands National Park (1901 Spinnaker Dr., Ventura CA 93001) Just off the coast of southern California lie the eight Channel Islands. Five of these islands, Anacapa, San Miguel, Santa Barbara, Santa Cruz and Santa Rosa, constitute the Channel Islands National Park. Activities on the islands include hiking, swimming, fishing, SCUBA diving and camping. All hiking must be done on established trails. Landing on

Santa Rosa and Santa Cruz is by permit only; contact Park Head-quarters for details. A new park visitor center in Ventura features "hands-on" exhibits, an observation tower and a film. The Visitor Center is open year-round from 8 A.M. to 5 P.M.

Island Packers Company, Box 993, Ventura CA 93002 provides public excursions to the islands. They accept reservations no sooner than 30 days in advance, and no later than 3 days before your trip. Call (805) 642-1393 for reservations.

Overnight camping is allowed only on Anacapa and Santa Barbara Islands and in designated sites only. A permit is required and an application may be obtained by writing the Park at the address listed above; or call (805) 644-8157.

Death Valley National Monument (Death Valley CA 92328)

The 3,000 square miles of Death Valley N.M. offer examples of each of the dozens of kinds of terrain and life that exemplify the word "desert," and even some probably not associated with the term. Here you will find badlands, saltwater springs and dry lakes as well as forested mountain peaks that are snow-capped part of the year and flowing springs of fresh water.

Resorts provide lodging and other commercial services at two locations in the Monument. Facilities are operated at Furnace Creek and Stovepipe Wells by Fred Harvey, Inc., Box 187, Death Valley CA 92328. At Stovepipe Wells, services are limited from May through October. Write to the address above for details.

The Death Valley backcountry has an unusual variety of rugged mountains and desert terrain. Backcountry users are not required to obtain a special permit, but registration at the Visitor Center or with a ranger is encouraged. Hiking is not recommended between May and October. Monument Headquarters has a great deal of helpful information available for use in planning a trip. Write for this free information.

Joshua Tree National Monument (Twentynine Palms CA 92277)

Located in beautiful California desert country, the Monument preserves a variety of plant and animal communities. It is the home of many creatures that have acquired special adaptations for survival in an arid environment. Elevations in the Monument range from 1,000' to nearly 6,000' in the Little San Bernardino Mountains. The weather is pleasant most of the year, though particularly so in spring and fall.

The Monument has 8 campgrounds available on a first-come, first-served basis. There are also 2 group campgrounds, which are available by reservation only. Campers must provide their own water and firewood or fuel. Motels, restaurants, etc. can be found in nearby cities.

Registration is required before entering the backcountry for an overnight or extended stay. Day hikers must register in a log provided for that purpose.

Point Reyes National Seashore (Point Reyes CA 94956)

This, the first protected National Seashore in the state, is located on the Marin County coast about 40 miles north of San Francisco. The area offers a variety of terrain from sandy beaches around Drakes Bay to the rugged woodlands of Inverness Ridge.

There are four hike-in campgrounds. Stays are limited to one night per campground and three nights per trip. Reservations are necessary and may be obtained in advance by contacting the Superintendent, Point Reyes National Seashore, Point Reyes CA 94956, (415) 663-1092.

Agua Tibia Wilderness

This 15,934-acre Wilderness is located on the west slope of Mt. Palomar in Cleveland National Forest. Elevations in the area vary from 1,700' in canyon bottoms to a 5,000' crest covered by a coniferous forest. Brush-covered slopes have been eroded and cut by intermittent streams to form deep canyons. Broad, sweeping panoramas can be seen from the upper ridges, not only of the immediate area, but of distant mountains and valleys, and occasionally the Pacific Ocean 40 miles west. There are about 25 miles of trail in the area, which is closed from July 1st each year to late November or early December due to the high fire hazard. Permits are required and may be obtained in person, by phone or by mail. Mail requests should be made at least two weeks in advance. Contact Cleveland National Forest or the Palomar Ranger District Office, 332 South Juniper Street, Escondido CA 92025, (619) 745-2421.

Caribou Wilderness

Located in Lassen National Forest and adjacent to Lassen Volcanic National Park, this 19,080-acre Wilderness is a gentle, rolling, forested plateau with many forest-fringed lakes. The lake area offers attractive camping spots and many of the larger ones are stocked with trout. The Wilderness can easily be explored by hiking its well-maintained trails, which are mostly on gentle slopes. Permits are required and may be obtained in person, by phone or by mail by contacting Lassen National Forest. There are also several ranger stations that provide permits. You can obtain their addresses and phone numbers by writing Lassen National Forest.

Cucamonga Wilderness

This is a rough and rugged land of sharp peaks and steep mountain-sides with elevations ranging from 5,000' to 9,000'. The 8,500 acres of this Wilderness are located in San Bernardino National Forest. The area has a capacity limit for day and for overnight use. Permit reservations can be obtained up to 90 days in advance by mail or in person from the Lytle Creek Ranger Station, Star Route, Box 100, Fontana CA 92335, (714) 887-2576. Phone reservations will be accepted on the day of use only. Telephone and in-person requests for permits can also be made at the Mt. Baldy Guard Station, Mt. Baldy CA, (714) 982-2829.

Desolation Wilderness

This 63,469-acre Wilderness lies immediately west of Lake Tahoe on both sides of the Sierra crest. It is one of the most northern of the glaciated High Sierra scenic lands. Elevations range from 6,500' to nearly 10,000'. This is fisherman's country, with many small streams and about 130 lakes, some as large as 900 acres. Because Desolation is easily accessible, very heavy use during the summer months has made a quota system for overnight users necessary. Only 700 overnight users per day are permitted to enter the area. Day-use permits are required but not subject to this quota. The quota system is in effect from June 15 through Labor Day each year. During the rest of the year no quotas are in effect. On the quota system, 50% of the permits may be reserved up to 90 days in advance by mail or in person. The remaining 50% will be allocated on a first-come, first-served basis. Contact Eldorado National Forest for a list of the trailheads, daily quota limits and additional information.

Dome Land Wilderness

Located in Sequoia National Forest, the 62,206 acres of this picturesque land are lightly used but easily accessible. The area is 70 miles east of Bakersfield on the southern edge of the Kern Plateau, between the South Fork and the main fork of the Kern River. It is an open, semi-arid area with elevations from 3,000' to 9,000', excellent for spring and fall backpacking. Erosion and weathering have left the area strewn with odd-shaped monolithic rock outcroppings, giving rise to the name "Dome Land." Permits are required and may be obtained in person, by mail or by phone from the Cannell Meadow Ranger District, Sequoia National Forest, Box 6, Kernville CA 93238, (619) 376-3781. Contact Sequoia National Forest for additional information.

Emigrant Wilderness

This is an area of broad expanses of glaciated granite, towering lava-capped peaks, numerous alpine lakes and meadows and deep, granite-walled canyons. Elevations vary from 5,200' to 11,570' atop Leavitt Peak. The 106,131 acres of the area are located in Stanislaus National Forest and are bordered on the south by Yosemite National Park. Permits are required and may be obtained in person or by phone from Stanislaus National Forest.

Golden Trout Wilderness

The 306,000 acres of this Wilderness are located in Inyo and Sequoia National Forests. The western part contains the Little Kern River, a large drainage basin capped by high, rugged mountains. The eastern part is an extension of the Kern Plateau. The area is northeast of Porterville and though the terrain varies, in general the area offers a gentle topography suitable for intermediate backpackers. Permits are required and may be obtained by mail or in person from the Tule River Ranger Sta-

tion, 32588 Highway 190, Porterville CA 93257, and the Mt. Whitney
Ranger Station, Box 8, Main Street, Lone Pine CA 93545, (619) 876-
4660. The Inyo National Forest has daily quotas in effect June 15–
Sept. 15. Write either National Forest for more information.

High Sierra Primitive Area

This extremely rough, mountainous area, located in Sequoia and Sierra
National Forests, is possibly the wildest in California. It includes Tehipite Valley, which approaches the scenic scale of Yosemite Valley. This
10,247-acre area is extremely rugged and has limited access and few
trails. It can be entered from Highway 180 via the Lewis Creek Trail or
the Deer Cove Creek Trail. Permits are required and may be obtained in
person, by phone or by mail from the Hume Lake Ranger District,
Sequoia National Forest, Miramonte CA 93641, (209) 336-2881. Write
either National Forest for additional information.

Hoover Wilderness

This small, 47,916-acre, extremely rugged wilderness is best suited to
the hardy backpacker. The trails are too high and rugged for easy horse
travel. Elevations range from 8,000' to 12,000'+. The best time for
backpacking is during July and August, but even then you should be
prepared for all kinds of weather including rain, summer blizzards, extreme cold and heavy winds. The southwest boundary of Hoover is
shared with Yosemite National Park. Permits, required to enter the
area, may be obtained in person or by mail from the Mono Lake Ranger
District, Highway 120, Box 10, Lee Vining CA 93541, (619) 647-6525,
or from the Bridgeport Ranger District, Highway 395 S., Bridgeport CA
93517, (619) 932-7070. For more information write either Toiyabe
(see Nevada National Forests) or Inyo National Forest.

John Muir Wilderness

Named for the famed naturalist, California's largest (503,478 acres)
Wilderness is considered by some to be the most inviting in America. It
extends along the crest of the Sierra Nevada from Mammoth Lakes
southward to the Mt. Whitney region. Rugged grandeur characterizes
this area. At the lower elevations there are gentle slopes along the
streams and lakes. Included are the headwaters of the South Fork of
the San Joaquin River, and the North Fork of the Kings. Thousands of
lakes are scattered throughout the area; they are well-stocked with
trout. Westside entry is through the Sierra National Forest and eastside
entry is through the Inyo National Forest. Both forests have a reservation system and entry limits. Permits are required for all trips. Entry
quotas are in effect during the heavy season. Mail or in-person reservations will be taken after March 1 by each district administering trailheads. Contact either National Forest for more details on permit
requirements.

Kaiser Wilderness

The 22,500-acre Kaiser Wilderness is located immediately north of Huntington Lake in Sierra National Forest, about 70 miles northeast of Fresno. Most of Kaiser Ridge is above timberline. Its high point is 10,320' Kaiser Peak, which provides a commanding view of a large part of the central Sierra Nevada. The southern part of this Wilderness rises gradually from the north shore of Huntington Lake through dense forests of red fir and Jeffrey pine to the alpine zone along the ridge. The northern part of the area contains all but two of the 20 small lakes in Kaiser Wilderness. This area has a reservation system and trailhead entry limit in effect. Permits are required and may be obtained in person at the Shaver Lake Ranger Station or the Eastwood Information Station, both located en route to the Wilderness. Or you may obtain your permit by writing the US Forest Service, Box 306, Shaver Lake CA 93664. Additional information on current conditions can be obtained at this same address or by phoning (209) 841-3311.

Marble Mountain Wilderness

Klamath National Forest contains this 214,390-acre Wilderness. It is a mild and mellow country, without the stark rock formations of most subalpine area. It is almost entirely forested, and easily traveled over mostly shaded and gently rising trails. Glaciated pockets at the heads of streams along the main ridges contain lakes hidden between the ridges, with adjacent meadows and timber pockets. Permits are required and can be obtained by mail, in person or by phone from Klamath National Forest.

Minarets Wilderness

This Wilderness lies north of the John Muir Wilderness along the Sierra Nevada crest. Elevations range from 7,000' to over 13,000'. This is rugged country with many trails, including the John Muir Trail, which crosses the Wilderness from Devils Postpile National Monument to Donohue Pass. The area affords unexcelled opportunities for experienced mountain climbers. Permits are required and there are trailhead quotas in effect from June 15 to September 15. Permit reservations will be accepted after March 1. Write to either Inyo or Sierra National Forest for more information.

Mokelumne Wilderness

Just west of the Sierra Nevada Crest, between highways 88 and 4, lies the 50,165-acre Mokelumne Wilderness. Barren Mokelumne Peak dominates the area. From its rocky prominences, the entire surroundings are revealed as lands of massive granite formations, carved and polished by wind and water. Along the eastern boundary lies a vast granite mass more than six miles square which reaches a height of over 10,000 feet. The Tahoe Yosemite Trail crosses the center of this Wilderness from north to south. Permits are required and can be obtained by contacting either Eldorado or Stanislaus National Forest.

Salmon-Trinity Alps Wilderness

Located along the headwaters of the Salmon and Trinity rivers in northern California, this is the third largest wilderness in the state. Its 287,337 acres contain high, rough mountain ridges and deep glacial canyons as well as 55 alpine lakes and many clear mountain streams. A 400-mile trail system extends throughout the area. Permits are required and information on how they can be obtained can be had by writing either Klamath or Shasta-Trinity National Forest.

San Gabriel Wilderness

Some of the most scenic country in southern California has been preserved in this 36,215-acre Wilderness. It is rough, rugged country with elevations that range from 1,600' to over 9,000'. Much of the region is covered with chaparral, but above 5,000' there is mixed pine and fir timber. Permits are required and can be obtained by phone, by mail or in person from Angeles National Forest. They can also supply you with additional information, as well as a list of five district ranger stations where permits may also be obtained.

San Gorgonio Wilderness

This 35,255-acre Wilderness covers the summit region of the San Bernardino Mountain Range, the highest range in southern California. Outstanding attractions are three peaks: San Gorgonio, San Bernardino and East San Bernardino, with their tremendous expanses of mountain and desert views. Small meadows and lakes offer contrast to wide reaches of barren rock. Generally water is available, but there are arid regions in the wilderness where water is not available. Only experienced hikers should stray from marked trails and then only after checking with Mill Creek Ranger Station for current conditions. Permits are required and the number issued each day is limited. For complete information on the permit reservation system, capacity limits, and current weather and hiking conditions for the area, contact San Bernardino National Forest or the Mill Creek Ranger Station, Route 1, Box 264, Mentone CA 92359, (714) 794-1123.

San Jacinto Wilderness

This area, high along the crest of the San Jacinto Mountains, contains some of the most spectacular mountain country in southern California. This wilderness consists of two parts: Mt. San Jacinto Wilderness State Park in the north and the National Forest Wilderness in the south. The northern part is the more spectacular. The views of the Mojave Desert and San Gorgonio Mountain, and the extreme contrasts from the alpine life zone to the Sonoran zone are among the most spectacular in California. Permits are necessary and reservations are required. There is also a limit on overnight users. For more detailed information on permits, reservations and capacity limits for the San Bernardino National Forest area write Idyllwild Ranger Station, Box 518, Idyllwild CA

92345, (714) 659-2117. For additional information on permits and reservations for the state park, contact Mt. San Jacinto Wilderness State Park, Box 308, Idyllwild CA 92349, (714) 659-2607.

San Rafael Wilderness

This Wilderness contains 149,170 acres of mountainous country in the San Rafael Mountains of west-central California. About 125 miles of trail give access to this scenic area where travel is by foot or horseback. Elevations range from 1,166' to over 6,800' at Big Pine Mountain. The Wilderness is open in the winter and spring months, but parts are closed in the summer and fall because of fire hazard. A permit is necessary and information on how to obtain it can be had by contacting Los Padres National Forest.

Santa Lucia Wilderness

This 21,250-acre Wilderness, located in Los Padres National Forest, consists of streamside vegetation and chaparral-covered slopes surrounding Lopez Canyon. The elevations range from 800' to 3,000' in the vicinity of the Hi Mountain Lookout. Permits are necessary and can be obtained from Los Padres National Forest Headquarters or at several other locations. Write Los Padres NF for additional information.

South Warner Wilderness

In the extreme northeastern corner of California lie the Warner Mountains, an isolated spur of the Cascade Range. Here is an area of alpine splendor, peaks, canyons, glacial and landslide lakes and picturesque mountain basins. The variety in topography and in vegetation, with patches of timber, grassy slopes and meadows, makes it an ideal area for a hiker in search of solitude. Tumbling streams, a few small lakes, many springs and associated meadows edged with aspens and bordered by rock and conifer patches contribute much to the beauty of the area. This 68,457-acre Wilderness is administered by Modoc National Forest. Permits are necessary and may be obtained by contacting Modoc National Forest.

Thousand Lakes Wilderness

This is a land of contrasting topography with a variety of vegetation. The area received its name from the many lakes in the lava "pot holes" formed during ancient eruptions of an extinct volcano whose remnants are known as Magee Peak. This 8,676' mountain in the southern part of the area is accessible by trail. There are seven major lakes in the Wilderness, all well-stocked with rainbow trout. This 16,335-acre area is managed by Lassen National Forest. Permits are required and can be obtained by writing the Forest headquarters.

Ventana Wilderness

The major portion of this 159,065-acre Wilderness lies on the coastward side of the Santa Lucia Range. At one point the area adjoins Pfeiffer-Big Sur State Park. The lower slopes are mostly chaparral-covered, with woodland and timber along many miles of all-year streams. Permits are necessary and may be obtained from the King City Ranger Station, 406 S. Mildred, King City CA 93930, (408) 385-5434. This Wilderness is located in Los Padres National Forest. Contact them for additional information.

Yolla Bolly-Middle Eel Wilderness

This 113,030-acre Wilderness is located in Mendocino and Shasta-Trinity National Forests. The North and South Yolla Bolly Mountains form the north and south parts of this wild and rugged country on the headwaters of the Middle Fork of the Eel River. Dense stands of pine and fir on ridges contrast with an extensive cover of chamise, manzanita and mountain mahogany at lower elevations. Permits are required to enter the area. They may be obtained at either National Forest headquarters or from any of six ranger districts. For their addresses contact the National Forest.

Bureau of Land Management (2800 Cottage Way, Sacramento CA 95825)

The BLM administers 16 million acres of public land in California, including 12½ million acres in the California desert. The nation's first National Conservation Area—the King Range on the north coast—is part of the BLM's domain, as are range and forest lands in the northern part of the state, oak and grass lands in the Coast Ranges and the Mother Lode, whitewater rivers, and the myriad landscapes of the vast desert area covering the southeastern one fourth of the state. Though all of the land is available for public use, much of it is not suitable for backpacking. The King Range is an exception.

The King Range lies along the northern coast of California. Extremely steep and rocky terrain forced the coastal highway route, State Highway 1, about 30 miles inland in the area of the King Range. This obstacle to transportation and settlement remains today as California's "Lost Coast."

The spectacular meeting of land and sea is certainly a dominant feature of the King Range National Conservation Area. However, it is also an area of mountain streams, trails and forests ideal for camping, hiking and fishing. There are four developed BLM recreation sites in addition to several water sources which serve primitive camps.

The 3,941-acre Chemise Mountain Area, within the King Range, is man aged for its wild qualities and to provide opportunities for solitude. I lies just south of Shelter Cove where nearly impassable cliffs rise from the ocean to great heights. Access to the area is by the 5-mile Chemise Mountain Trail, which has been designated as a National Recreation Trail.

State Parks

There are over 200 parks in the California State Park System and back packing is possible in many of them. Of particular interest is Anza-Borrego Desert State Park, located about 85 miles northeast of San Diego. Unlimited primitive camping is possible within the park's half million acres. Also of interest to the backpacker are Mt. San Jacinto State Park, Henry W. Coe State Park, and Pfeiffer-Big Sur State Park.

Most campsites can be reserved in advance through Ticketron outlets. There is a reservation charge as well as a campsite fee; both must be paid when the reservation is made.

The California Department of Parks and Recreation publishes a large brochure that briefly describes what facilities and activities can be expected in all the state parks. It costs $1, including postage, and is available from the Distribution Center, Department of Parks and Recreation, Box 2390, Sacramento CA 95811.

Another area of interest to the backpacker is the *Skyline to the Sea Trail*, which connects Castle Rock State Park with Big Basin Redwoods State Park. The parks are located in the Santa Cruz Mountains and, due to the efforts of the Sempervirens Fund, there are now more than 60 miles of trails in and between the two parks. The *Skyline to the Sea Trail* is the principal link in a proposed trail network connecting several state and county parks and linking the skyline to the sea in a trail system of state-wide significance.

For more information on trail camp registration, permits and maps of the trail system, contact Big Basin Redwoods State Park, Big Basin CA 95006, (408) 338-6132.

California Office of Tourism (Dept. HC, 1030 13th St., Suite 200, Sacramento CA 94814)

The California Office of Tourism publishes a 16-page booklet entitled *Hiking and Camping.* This publication contains information on making reservations in the state and national park systems, packing with animals, obtaining a fishing license and sources of additional information for camping and backpacking areas in California. For a free copy of the booklet, send a self-addressed, stamped business envelope to the California Office of Tourism at the above address.

National Forests

Angeles National Forest
150 S. Los Robles Ave. Room 300
Pasadena CA 91101
(213) 684-0350 or
(213) 577-0050

Cleveland National Forest
880 Front St.
Room 6-S-5
San Diego CA 92188
(619) 293-5050

Eldorado National Forest
100 Forni Road
Placerville CA 95667
(916) 622-5061

Inyo National Forest
873 N. Main St.
Bishop CA 93514
(619) 873-5841

Klamath National Forest
1312 Fairlane Rd.
Yreka CA 96097
(916) 842-6131

Lassen National Forest
707 Nevada St.
Susanville CA 96130
(916) 257-2151

Los Padres National Forest
42 Aero Camino
Goleta CA 93017
(805) 968-1578

Mendocino National Forest
420 E. Laurel St.
Willows CA 95988
(916) 934-3316

Modoc National Forest
441 N. Main St.
Alturas CA 96101
(916) 233-5811

Plumas National Forest
Box 1500
Quincy CA 95971
(916) 283-2050

San Bernardino National Forest
144 N. Mt. View Ave.
San Bernardino CA 92408
(714) 383-5588

Sequoia National Forest
900 W. Grand Ave.
Porterville CA 93257
(209) 784-1500

Shasta-Trinity National Forest
2400 Washington Ave.
Redding CA 96001
(916) 246-5222

Sierra National Forest
Federal Bldg.
1130 "O" St.
Fresno CA 93721
(209) 487-5155

Six Rivers National Forest
507 "F" St.
Eureka CA 95501
(707) 442-1721

Stanislaus National Forest
19777 Greenley Road
Sonora CA 95370
(209) 532-3671

Tahoe National Forest
Highway 49
Nevada City CA 95959
(916) 265-4531

ALASKA AND HAWAII

Alaska

Alaska is a breathtakingly big land of truly rugged wilderness. Within its
586,400 square miles are 3 million lakes, 24 active volcanoes and half
the world's glaciers. For general information about the areas that have
been designated by the National Park Service for backpacking, write to
Alaska National Parks and Monuments Association, 540 W. 5th Ave.,
Anchorage AK 99501. Another good source of general information,
since most of the Alaskan wilderness is reachable only by air or boat, is

Exploration Holidays and Cruises, 1500 Metropolitan Park Bldg., Olive Way at Boren Ave., Seattle WA 98101. *All* backpacking trips will require that you make ample preparation and take more than the usual precautions. Write directly to the areas listed here for details.

Denali National Park and Preserve (Box 9, McKinley Park AK 99755)
At the northern edge of the continent, close to the Arctic Circle, rises mammoth Mount McKinley; at 20,320' it is North America's highest peak, dominating this immense wild area of Alaska. It is by far the most impressive feature of the Alaska Range, a curved chain of mountains that stretches 580 miles across the lower third of Alaska, acting as a natural land barrier between Anchorage on the coastal lowlands and Alaska's interior to the north. Within the park are towering mountains, alpine glaciers and gentle rolling lowlands crossed by wide rivers.

There are no established backcountry trails in the Park. All travel is cross-country, across tundra or through spruce forest or bushy areas. During summer there are 16–20 hours of daylight, and typically summer weather is cool, wet and windy. Best hiking is from mid-June to early September. A tent and a mosquito barrier are backpacking essentials.

A backcountry permit is required for all overnight trips, and all permits are issued on a first-come, first-served basis at the Riley Creek Information Center. Assistance in route planning is also available here.

The Park has seven campgrounds, but only one is open year-round. Sites at the campgrounds are available on a first-come, first-served basis, but you must still register at the Riley Creek Information Center when you first arrive in the Park.

The Denali National Park Hotel has 98 rooms and 84 railroad-sleeping-car accommodations, as well as meals, groceries, auto service and bus transportation. For reservations contact Outdoor World Ltd., Denali Park AK 99755, (907) 683-2215 in summer; (907) 278-1122 in winter.

Katmai National Monument (Box 7, King Salmon AK 99613)
No roads lead to this vast area of glaciers, forests, island-studded lakes, fjords, bays, beaches and volcanoes, but daily air flights connect Anchorage with King Salmon.

There are few trails (except those made by bears) but good routes are generally located along river bars, lake shores and gravel ridges. Because biting insects thrive between mid-June and mid-August, hiking is at its best from late August to early September. By mid-September temperatures begin to drop below freezing and snowstorms may occur.

A backcountry permit, required for hiking in Katmai, can be obtained at the Ranger Station at Brooks Camp or at Park Headquarters in King Salmon.

Glacier Bay National Monument (Gustavus AK 99826)

This rugged wilderness of 4400 square miles is situated in southeastern Alaska. There are no roads to Glacier Bay, so Gustavus must be reached by boat or airplane (daily service from Juneau). Bus service operates between Gustavus and Bartlett Cove, the Monument's headquarters. Most backpackers get up-bay by means of the daily tour boat, which runs the 40 miles from Bartlett Cove into Muir Inlet, where dropoff points have been established.

Glacier Bay has no trails or established campsites other than at Bartlett Cove. The terrain ranges from recently glaciated, barren landscapes to areas covered by dense growths of alder. The climate is damp and cool—weather is best during May and June, tending to get wetter by late summer and fall. Snow persists on the ridges and low peaks until late summer. Backpackers and kayakers should register at the Bartlett Cove Ranger Station.

Bureau of Land Management

The BLM manages more than 174,000,000 acres of public land in Alaska, most of it undeveloped and not easily accessible. Because Alaska is undergoing rapid changes in land ownership and management (for example, some 44,000,000 acres are currently being transferred from the federal government to Alaska Natives under the 1971 Alaska Native Claims Settlement Act) it is always best to check with the BLM on the land status before you begin travel in the backcountry. For more information on camping in BLM campgrounds, using their "Public Use Cabins" or camping in undeveloped sites, write the BLM headquarters at 701 C Street, Box 13, Anchorage AK 99513, (907) 271-5555.

State Parks

Alaska's State Park system, while the youngest in the country, has grown in acreage to become America's largest State Park system, with nearly 3,000,000 acres of land under its jurisdiction. All facilities are on a first-come, first-served basis, and reservations are not required. A $10 yearly fee is charged for the use of park facilities. For more information contact the Division of Parks, 619 Warehouse Dr., Suite 210, Anchorage AK 99501, (907) 276-2653.

Forest Service

The United States Department of Agriculture's Forest Service manages 5.9 million acres of land for recreation, wildlife, water, timber, minerals and other resources within the boundaries of the Chugach National Forest in south-central Alaska. In this land of multiple uses, the Forest Service maintains 16 developed campgrounds, 36 accessible public-use cabins, 181 miles of hiking trails, the 8,600-acre Portage Glacier Recreation Center and several picnic areas and further extends to the recreationist the chance to hunt, fish, canoe, kayak, ski, snowmobile, bird-watch, sightsee, pan for gold or even search for the wily iceworm. For

general information about facilities and recreational opportunities on
the forest contact the Chugach National Forest. For detailed information on Portage Glacier or to make cabin reservations write: Anchorage
Ranger District, P.O. Box 10-469, Huffman Business Park, Bldg. C.,
Anchorage AK 99511.

National Forests

Chugach National Forest
2221 E. Northern Lights Blvd.
Suite 238
Anchorage AK 99508
(907) 279-4485

Tongass National Forest
Ketchikan Area
Federal Building
Ketchikan AK 99901
(907) 225-3101

Tongass National Forest
Stikine Area
Box 309
Petersburg AK 99833
(907) 772-4266

Tongass National Forest
Chatham Area
Box 1980
Sitka AK 99835
(907) 747-6671

Hawaii

Hawaii has many backpacking opportunities other than those at its two
national parks. There are various agencies you can write to for information on trails and campsites that they maintain, and they are listed here
by island.

Hawaii: Division of State Parks
PO Box 936
75 Aupuni St.
Hilo HI 96720

Dept. of Parks & Recreation, County of Hawaii
25 Aupuni St.
Hilo HI 96720

Kauai: Division of State Parks
3060 Eiwa St., Room 208
Lihue HI 96766

Dept. of Parks & Recreation, County of Kauai
4396 Rice Street
Lihue HI 96766

Maui: Division of State Parks
Box 1049
State Office Building
Wailuku HI 96793

Dept. of Parks & Recreation, County of Maui
County Building
Wailuku HI 96793

Oahu: Division of State Parks
           1151 Punchbowl St., Room 310
           Honolulu HI 96813

           Dept. of Parks & Recreation
           City & County of Honolulu
           Honolulu Municipal Building
           650 South King St.
           Honolulu HI 96813

           Division of Forestry
           1151 Punchbowl St., Room 325
           Honolulu HI 96813

Hawaii Volcanoes National Park (Hawaii Volcanoes National Park HI 96718)

This Park was created primarily to preserve the natural setting of the big island's two volcanoes, Mauna Loa and Kilauea. The Park extends from Mauna Loa, in the central part of the island, to the seacoast near Kalapana. Lush rainforests, raw craters and great areas of devastation can be viewed from Crater Rim Drive or from the 11-mile Crater Rim Trail. The Mauna Loa Trail begins at an elevation of 6,662' and rises gradually for 18 miles, ending at the Summit Cabin at an elevation of 13,680'.

Hikers must register at either the Kilauea or Wahaula visitor center when beginning a trip. The Park is a geologically active area and it is important for rangers to know the location of backcountry users. Sturdy hiking shoes are strongly recommended because of the rough lava surfaces. The National Park Service maintains two patrol cabins on Mauna Loa that may be used free by hikers; a cabin may not be reserved in advance.

A hotel on the rim of Kilauea Caldera is open year-round. For reservations, write Volcano House, Hawaii Volcanoes National Park HI 96718. There are also three campgrounds within the park. Sites cannot be reserved in advance, and your stay is limited to seven days.

Haleakala National Park (Box 369, Makawao, Maui HI 96768)

This National Park was created to preserve the outstanding geologic features of Haleakala Crater. The Park stretches from the 10,023' summit of Mt. Haleakala eastward to the Kipahulu coastal area. Haleakala is a prime example of a dormant volcano in various stages of erosion. The backcountry wilderness is comprised of majestic cinder cones, stark lava fields and pockets of lush vegetation.

There are 32 miles of hiking trails. A backcountry camping permit is required and can be obtained at Park headquarters. Campsites cannot be reserved, being operated on a first-come, first-served basis. There is a limit of two consecutive nights in any one campsite. Three small, primitive cabins are maintained in Haleakala Crater, reachable by trail only; they can be reserved only by mail, and cabin assignments are chosen by lot.

There are no stores, service stations, hotels or food services within the Park, but these facilities are available from 16-30 miles away.

Long and Famous Trails

For some backpackers, nothing can beat the thrill of a successful trek on a long and demanding trail. A long-distance trek, be it on a 100-mile segment of the Appalachian Trail or on the entire length of the 2560-mile Pacific Crest Trail, can offer a very special wilderness experience with many pleasures and satisfactions. It can offer a unique sense of *journey* in the wilderness and, afterward, a real sense of accomplishment in having completed that journey.

However, there can be other features of a long backpacking trip: logistical nightmares, unimagined physical discomfort, extreme wear and tear on equipment, and other unforeseen discouragements. You can minimize these possibilities by planning your trip carefully and knowing what to expect in terrain, weather and trail conditions. If you are planning to hike any of these long and famous trails, be sure to contact the organizations we have listed. They can give you the kind of help and information you need for a successful expedition.

A new organization known as "Long Distance Hikers" was founded in October 1982. The group promotes long-distance hiking and encourages communication among those who have hiked over 2,000 miles and those who would like to take long treks. Their newsletter carries classified ads for those looking for hiking partners for long and short hiking trips. For information on membership and additional information contact Warren Doyle, Box C, Pipestem WV 25979.

Where we mention clubs and guidebooks by name, addresses are listed in the "Hiking Clubs" and publishers are listed in the "Trail Guides" section of the book.

The Pacific Crest Trail. This 2560-mile trail, which goes from the Mexican border in southern California through California, Oregon and Washington to the Canadian border in Washington, offers an unparalleled challenge in long-distance backpacking. Two regional offices of the Forest Service can give you trail information—the Regional Forester of the Pacific Northwest Region (319 SW Pine St., Portland OR 97208) and the Regional Forester of the Pacific Southwest Region (630 Sansome St., San Francisco CA 94111). Hiking a long portion of this trail requires careful planning, and you can get some help from Pacific Crest Trail Conference (Box 1907, Santa Ana CA 92702). Contact them to find out what they offer. In addition, Wilderness Press publishes two excellent guidebooks, a California volume and an Oregon & Washington volume, to the entire trail, and Signpost Publications offers a PCT Hike Planning Guide (see under "Washington" in the Trail Guides section).

The Appalachian Trail. This 2000-mile trail goes from Mt. Katahdin in central Maine to Springer Mountain in northern Georgia. Three very large organizations can give you a great deal of help in planning a long-distance trek: the Appalachian Mountain Club in Massachusetts, the Appalachian Trail Conference in West Virginia and the Potomac Appalachian Trail Club in Washington D.C. They also publish excellent guidebooks and maps to different parts of the trail.

The Long Trail. For information on this 255-mile trail through the Green Mountains of Vermont, contact Green Mountain National Forest, The Green Mountain Club, and the Vermont Travel Division (134 State St., Montpelier VT 05602). The Green Mountain Club also publishes a guidebook to the trail.

The Florida Trail. There is now legislation pending in Congress that would make this a National Scenic Trail; that legislation is expected to pass. Much of this 1300-mile trail is still in the planning stages, but 800 miles have already been completed. The trail will run north from Everglades National Park, through Big Cypress Swamp, the Kissimmee Prairie, Withlocoochee State Forest, Ocala National Forest, Osceola National Forest and Black Water River State Forest. For information, write to the Florida Trail Association, Box 13708, Gainesville FL 32604.

Benton MacKaye Trail. This trail, named for the "father" of the Appalachian Trail, may soon provide the longest loop trail in the southeast US. The 238-mile trail is planned to circle through Georgia, North Carolina and Tennessee. The Forest Service has approved the route in Georgia; approval is still pending for the proposed route through North Carolina and Tennessee. At the time of writing, 43 miles of blazed, walkable trail exist. They are described in a publication available from the Chattahoochee National Forest headquarters in Georgia. For additional information contact the Benton MacKaye Trail Association, Box 53271, Atlanta GA 30305.

North Country Trail. This 3,200-mile trail was designated a National Scenic Trail in March 1980. The trail begins at Crown Point, NY and swings more than 3,000 miles through seven states to meet up with the Lewis and Clark Trail in North Dakota, near Lake Sacajawea. For more information on the development of this trail, write North Country Trail Association, Box 311, White Cloud MI 49349.

The Continental Divide Trail. This partly completed 3100-mile route extends from near the Mexican border in southwestern New Mexico northward generally along the Continental Divide to the Canadian border in Glacier National Park. Guidebooks are available to the Montana, Idaho, Wyoming and Northern Colorado parts of the trail.

The Pacific Northwest Trail. This trail extends approximately 1200 miles from the Continental Divide in Glacier National Park, Montana, to the Pacific Ocean beach of Olympic National Park, Washington. The route takes you through Flathead and Kootenai National Forests in Montana, Kaniksu National Forest in Idaho; and Colville National Forest, Okanogan National Forest, Pasayten Wilderness Area, Ross Lake National Recreation Area, North Cascades National Park, Olympic National Forest, and Olympic National Park in Washington. A guidebook to the trail will be published late in 1983. For more information on helping build the trail and membership in the PNWT Association send a self-addressed, stamped envelope to: Pacific Northwest Trail Assoc., Box 1048, Seattle WA 98111, (206) 525-3591.

The John Muir Trail. This very popular and well-known trail (most of it now a segment of the Pacific Crest Trail) travels a 210-mile length of the High Sierra between Mt. Whitney and Yosemite Valley. Guidebooks to the trail are available from Wilderness Press and Sierra Club Books.

The Tahoe-Yosemite Trail. This 180-mile mountain route goes from Meeks Bay on Lake Tahoe to Tuolumne Meadows in Yosemite National Park, passing through popular Desolation Wilderness and then through some of the Sierra's less-visited high country. Wilderness Press publishes a guidebook to this trail.

Of the trails that we have listed here, four have been designated National Scenic Trails: the Pacific Crest Trail, the Appalachian Trail, the Continental Divide Trail and the North Country Trail. There are also now a total of five National Historic Trails: the Lewis and Clark Trail, the Oregon Trail, the Mormon Trail, the Iditarod Trail and the Overmountain Victory Trail. More than a dozen other trails are under study by the National Park Service and may eventually receive some official designation. These include the Daniel Boone Trail, the Desert Trail, the Nez Perce Trail and the William Bartram Trail.

Kindred Spirits

Joining an outdoor club can be a good way to meet other people who share your interests. Some of the organizations listed here may be more involved in local conservation efforts than others, but in all you will find people who enjoy the outdoors and who know a great deal about local trails and backpacking opportunities. (Some groups even have trail guides and maps not available elsewhere.)

Write directly to these groups to find out more about who they are and what they do. In the National category of Hiking Organizations, we have listed those groups that have a wider scope than the local clubs; most of these national groups are made up of smaller hiking clubs. The local groups, which we have listed by region and by state, vary considerably in size and scope. Some, like The Mountaineers in Washington, are quite large and have a wide range of involvements, while others, like the member groups of the Appalachian Trail Club, may be primarily involved in local trail construction and maintenance. National organizations are listed alphabetically, and regional clubs are listed here by region, by state and then by city.

In addition to the national conservation groups we have listed, there are many local citizens' groups dedicated to preserving wilderness and wildlife close to home. A complete listing of virtually *all* conservation groups can be found in the National Wildlife Federation's "1983 Conservation Directory." It can be ordered for $10.55 (includes postage) from: National Wildlife Federation, 1412 Sixteenth St. NW, Washington DC 20036.

Hiking Clubs

When writing to any of the clubs listed below, please include a self-addressed, stamped business envelope for their reply. Many of the clubs operate on a limited budget and just can't afford the postage to reply to the hundreds of requests they get for information each year.

If you have difficulty contacting any of the associate clubs listed under our regional headings, you should write the main office, if listed under our national heading.

National

The American Hiking Society
1701 18th St. NW
Washington DC 20009

American Historical Trails
P.O. Box 810
Washington DC 20044

American Youth Hostels, Inc.
National Administrative Offices
1332 I St. NW, Suite 800
Washington DC 20005

Appalachian Mountain Club
5 Joy St.
Boston MA 02108

Appalachian Trail Conference
Box 807
Harpers Ferry WV 25425

Boy Scouts of America
1325 Walnut Hill
Irving TX 75062

Federation of Western Outdoor Clubs
1516 Melrose
Seattle WA 98122

The International Backpackers
    Association, Inc.
P.O. Box 85
Lincoln Center ME 04458

Keystone Trails Assoc.
Box 251
Cogan Station PA 17728

National Campers and Hikers
    Assoc., Inc.
7172 Transit Rd.
Buffalo NY 14221

National Trails Council
c/o Forrest House
33 Knollwood Drive
E. Longmeadow MA 01028

New England Trail Conference
Box 145
Weston VT 05161

Potomac Appalachian Trail Club
1718 N St. NW
Washington DC 20036

Sierra Club
530 Bush St.
San Francisco CA 94108

Regional

New England

AMC Berkshire Chapter
Alberta Stutsman
23 Brookside Dr.
Wilbraham MA 01095

AMC Boston Chapter
Dick Siegel
201 Russet Rd.
Brookline MA 02146

AMC Connecticut Chapter
G. C. Hardy
74 Avondale Rd.
Manchester CT 06040

AMC Maine Chapter
James Thorne
RR1 Box 108
Yarmouth ME 04096

AMC New Hampshire Chapter
Harry Westcott
Pinewood Circle
Walpole NH 03608

AMC New York Chapter
(212) 736-9158

AMC Catskill Chapter
Bob Abromaitis
(518) 371-4236

AMC Massachusetts Chapter
Vicki Fitzgerald
220 High Street
Duxbury MA 02332

AMC Vermont Chapter
Bruce McGarry
RFD 2
Chester VT 05143

AMC Worcester Chapter
Carol Kanis
535 Harvard Rd.
Lancaster MA 01523

AMC Narragansett Chapter
Roy Benoit
102 Greenwich Ave.
Warwick RI 02886

American Youth Hostels
Greater Boston Council
1020 Commonwealth Ave.
Boston MA 02215

American Youth Hostels
Yankee Council
Box 10392
West Hartford CT 06110

American Youth Hostels
Hudson-Mohawk Council
Box 6343
Albany NY 12206

American Youth Hostels
Metropolitan New York Council
132 Spring St.
New York NY 10012

American Youth Hostels
Northern New York Council
65 Park St.
Malone NY 12953

American Youth Hostels
Syracuse Council
459 Westcott St.
Syracuse NY 13210

Sierra Club, New England Chapter
3 Joy St.
Boston MA 02108

Sierra Club, Connecticut Chapter
118 Oak St.
Hartford CT 06106

Sierra Club, Atlantic Chapter
196 Morton Ave.
Albany NY 12202

Green Mountain Club
45 Park St.
Rutland VT 05701

Connecticut Forest and Park Assoc.
1010 Main St.
Box 389
East Hartford CT 06108

Taconic Hiking Club
50 Newark St.
Cohoes NY 12047

Adirondack Mountain Club
172 Ridge St.
Glen Falls NY 12801

Finger Lakes Trail Conference
22 Sturbridge Lane
Pittsford NY 14534

North Country Trail Assoc.
c/o Lance Field
Box 85
Lincoln Center ME 04458

Mid-Atlantic

AMC Delaware Valley Chapter
(215) 328-2799

Sierra Club, Potomac Chapter
c/o Hudson
7276 Larrup Ct.
Alexandria VA 22310

Sierra Club, Pennsylvania Chapter
Box 135
Cogan Station PA 17728

Sierra Club, Old Dominion Chapter
c/o Holcomb
Rt 2 Box 385
Blacksburg VA 24060

Sierra Club, New Jersey Chapter
360 Nassau St.
Princeton NJ 08540

American Youth Hostels
Delaware Valley Council
35 South 3rd
Philadelphia PA 19106

American Youth Hostels
Pittsburg Council
6300 Fifth Avenue
Pittsburg PA 15232

American Youth Hostels
Potomac Area Council
1332 I St. NW, Suite 451
Washington DC 20005

Allegheny Outdoor Club
c/o Ruth Samuelson
205 Pickering
Sheffield PA 16347

Allentown Hiking Club
c/o Bill Sandt
2026 Henderson St.
Bethlehem PA 18017

Alpine Club of Williamsport
Box 501
Williamsport PA 17701

Batona Hiking Club
c/o Oreste Unti
600 E. Phil-Ellena St.
Philadelphia PA 19119

Beaver Creek Outing Club
c/o Robert Shannon
1640 Shannon Dr.
Harrisburg PA 17112

Blue Mountain Academy Outdoor Club
c/o Robert Egbert
Blue Mountain Academy
Hamburg PA 19526

Blue Mountain Eagle Climbing Club
Box 3523
Reading PA 19605

Brandywine Valley Outing Club
Box 7033
Wilmington DE 19803

Chester County Trail Club
c/o Clair Piersol
16 Lloyd Ave.
Downingtown PA 19335

Chestnut Hill Academy
c/o Edward Stainton
500 W. Wilson Ave.
Philadelphia PA 19118

Flood City 4-H Backpackers
R.D.#2, Box 71
Johnstown PA 15904

Horse-Shoe Trail Club
c/o Richard Harris
Box 126
Mt. Gretna PA 17064

Kabob Hiking Club
c/o Donald Koones
206 Lopaz Rd.
Harrisburg PA 17112

Lancaster Hiking Club
Box 6037
Lancaster PA 17603

Lebanon Valley Hiking Club
c/o David Gontz
1138 S. Green St.
Londonderry Farms
Palmyra PA 17078

McCaskey Hiking Club
c/o Betty Beck
McCaskey High School
225 W. Orange St.
Lancaster PA 17604

Mason-Dixon Trail System
118 Rustic Drive
Newark DE 19713

Mountain Club of Maryland
c/o Ronald Bowers
1343 Huntover Dr.
Odenton MD 21113

National Campers & Hikers Assoc.
PA State Association
c/o Jack Koons
2347 N. George St.
York PA 17402

Penn State Outing Club
Hiking Division
Room #4, Intramural Bldg.
University Park PA 16802

Philadelphia Trail Club
c/o Elizbeth Perry
9 Hathaway Circle
Wynnewood PA 19096

Reading Community Hiking Club
c/o Larry Witman
210 Mercer St.
Reading PA 19601

Shady Side Academy Backpacking Club
c/o John Thrope
423 Fox Chapel Rd.
Pittsburg PA 15238

Springfield Trail Club
c/o Wilma Flaig
Box 441
Media PA 19063

Susquehanna Appalachian Trail Club
c/o Robert Keck
67 W. Caracas Ave.
Hershey PA 17033

Susquehanna Trailers Hiking Club
c/o Joe Gmiter
339 Ridge Ave.
Kingston PA 18704

Susquehannock Trail Club
c/o Curt Weinhold
704 Southeast St.
Coudersport PA 16915

Warrior Trail Association
502 County Office Building
Waynesburg PA 15370

Wilmington Trail Club
Box 1184
Wilmington DE 19899

York Hiking Club
c/o Ronald Gray
89 W. Main St.
Dallastown PA 17313

Southeast

Sierra Club, Alabama Chapter
c/o Angermann
1718 Hillcrest Rd. NE
Cullman AL 35055

Sierra Club, Arkansas Chapter
Box 252
Fayetteville AR 72701

Sierra Club, Chattahoochee Chapter
c/o Mayhew
Box 38131
Atlanta GA 33034

Sierra Club, Cumberland Chapter
c/o Graddy
Rt 1, Hedden Rd.
Versailles KY 40383

Sierra Club, Delta Chapter
111 S. Hennessey St.
New Orelans LA 70119

Sierra Club, Florida Chapter
c/o Morris
Box 627
Sarasota FL 33578

Sierra Club, Mississippi Chapter
Box 4335
513 N State St.
Jackson MS 39216

Sierra Club, North Carolina Chapter
Box 2860
Winston Salem NC 27102

Sierra Club, South Carolina Chapter
Box 12112
Columbia SC 29211

Sierra Club, Tennessee Chapter
c/o McCaleb
100 Colonial Dr.
Hendersonville TN 37075

Midwest

American Youth Hostels
Columbus Council
103 W. Park St., Apt B
Westerville OH 43081

American Youth Hostels
Erie-Ana Council
304 N. Church St.
Bowling Green OH 43402

American Youth Hostels
Lima Council
Box 173
Lima OH 45802

American Youth Hostels
Toledo Council
3440 Larwin Dr.
Toledo OH 43623

American Youth Hostels
Tri-State Council
5400 Lanius Lane
Cincinnati OH 45224

American Youth Hostels
Metropolitan Chicago Council
3712 N. Clark St.
Chicago IL 60613

American Youth Hostels
Metropolitan Detroit Council
3024 Collidge
Berkley MI 48072

American Youth Hostels
Western Michigan Council
1013 West Burton
Grand Rapids MI 49509

American Youth Hostels
Wisconsin Council
1417 Wauwatosa Ave., Room 102
Wauwatosa WI 53213

American Youth Hostels
Minnesota Council
475 Cedar St.
St. Paul MN 55101

American Youth Hostels
Northwest Indiana Council
8231 Lake Shore Dr.
Gary IN 46403

American Youth Hostels
Northeast Iowa Council
139 West Greene St.
Box 10
Postville IA 52162

American Youth Hostels
Ozark Area Council
5400 A Southwest
St. Louis MO 63139

American Youth Hostels
Nebraskaland Council
12637 N St.
Omaha NE 68137

Sierra Club, Dacotah Chapter
Box 1624
Rapid City SD 57701

Sierra Club, Great Lakes Chapter
53 W. Jackson, Suite 1064
Chicago IL 60604

Sierra Club, Hoosier Chapter
Box 40275
Indianapolis IN 46240

Sierra Club, Iowa Chapter
The Thoreau Center
3500 Kingman Blvd.
Des Moines IA 50311

Sierra Club, John Muir Chapter
111 King St.
Madison WI 53703

Sierra Club, Kansas Chapter
RR 2, Box 170
5640 S 103rd St. E
Derby KS 67037

Sierra Club, Mackinac Chapter
135 Linden
East Lansing MI 48823

Sierra Club, Nebraska Chapter
1602 Military Ave.
Omaha NE 68111

Sierra Club, North Star Chapter
2929 4th Ave. South #N
Minneapolis MN 55408

Sierra Club, Ohio Chapter
65 South 4th St.
Columbus OH 43215

Sierra Club, Ozark Chapter
Box 12424
Olivette MO 63132

Buckeye Trail Association
Box 254
Worthington OH 43085

Cleveland Hiking Club
c/o Emily Gregor
6502 Olde York Rd.
Cleveland OH 44130

Southwest

American Youth Hostels
Arizona State Council
14049 N. 38th Place
Phoenix AZ 85032

Sierra Club, Lone Star Chapter
Box 1931
Austin TX 78767

Sierra Club, Oklahoma Chapter
c/o Zoellick
1912 State Lane
Stillwater OK 74074

Sierra Club, Rio Grande Chapter
1709 Paseo de Peralta
Santa Fe NM 87501

Sierra Club, Grand Canyon Chapter
c/o Colton
1355E East Fort Lowell
Tucson AZ 85719

Mountain

American Youth Hostels
Rocky Mountain Council
1107 12th St.
Boulder CO 80306

Sierra Club, Montana Chapter
c/o Curtis
9650 Grant Creek Rd.
Missoula MT 59802

Sierra Club, Rocky Mountain Chapter
2239 E. Colfax #206
Denver CO 80206

Sierra Club, Utah Chapter
Utah Environmental Center
Box 8393
Salt Lake City UT 84108

Sierra Club, Wyoming Chapter
Box 376
Kaycee WY 82639

Sierra Club, Toiyabe Chapter
Box 8096, University Station
Reno NV 89507

Colorado Mountain Club
2530 West Alameda
Denver CO 80219

Wasatch Mountain Club
1228 Bryon Ave.
Salt Lake City UT 84105

American Wilderness Alliance
4260 E. Evans Ave.
Denver CO 80222

Idaho Alpine Club
Box 2885
Idaho Falls ID 83401

Montana Wilderness Assoc.
Box 635
Helena MT 59601

Rocky Mountaineers
Box 4262
Missoula MT 59807

Pacific Northwest

American Youth Hostels
Oregon State Council
4212 SW Primrose St.
Portland OR 97219

American Youth Hostels
Washington State Council
1431 Minor Ave.
Seattle WA 98101

Sierra Club, Northern Rockies Chapter
Box 424
Spokane WA 99210

Sierra Club, Oregon Chapter
2637 SW Water St.
Portland OR 97201

Sierra Club, Cascade Chapter
c/o Sabol
17 Oak Park Dr. SW
Tacoma WA 98499

Admiralty Audubon Society
Box 666
Port Townsend WA 98368

Angora Hiking Club
Box 12
Astoria OR 97103

Boeing Employees Alpine Club
Box 3707
Mail Stop 4H-96
Seattle WA 98124

Cascade Wilderness Club
Box 1547
Yakima WA 98227

Cascadians, Inc.
Box 2201
Yakima WA 98902

Chemeketans
360½ State St.
Salem OR 97301

Hobnailers, Inc.
Box 1256
Spokane WA 99210

Hood River Crag Rats
4720 Kenwood Dr.
Hood River OR 97031

Intermountain Alpine Club
Box 505
Richland WA 99352

Klahane Club
Box 494
Port Angeles WA 98362

Mazamas
909 NW 19th Ave.
Portland OR 97209

Mount Baker Club
Box 73
Bellingham WA 98227

Mt. St. Helens Club
Box 843
Longview WA 98632

Mountaineers
719 Pike St.
Seattle WA 98101

Obsidians, Inc.
Box 322
Eugene OR 97440

Olympians, Inc.
Box 401
Hoquiam WA 98550

Olympic Peninsula Audubon Society
Box 502
Sequim WA 98383

Palouse Audubon Society
c/o Muriel Lamb
NW 800 Clifford
Pullman WA 99167

Ptarmigans
Box 1821
Vancouver WA 98668

Santiam Alpine Club
Box 1041
Salem OR 97308

Seattle Audubon Society
619 Joshua Green Bldg.
Seattle WA 98101

Skagit Alpine Club
Box 513
Mt. Vernon WA 98273

Spokane Mountaineers
Box 1013
Spokane WA 99210

Summit Alpine Club
c/o Mick Holt
6542 4th NE #2
Seattle WA 98115

Trails Club of Oregon
Box 1243
Portland OR 97207

Wanderers
c/o D. Clinton
5102 Mud Bay Road NW
Olympia WA 98502

Washington Alpine Club
Box 352
Seattle WA 98111

Washington Kayak Club
Box 24264
Seattle WA 98124

Pacific Northwest Trail Assoc.
Box 1048
Seattle WA 98111

California

American Youth Hostels
Central California Council
Box 28148
San Jose CA 95159

American Youth Hostels
Golden Gate Council
Building 240, Ft. Mason
San Francisco CA 94123

American Youth Hostels
Los Angeles Council
1502 Palos Verdes Dr., N.
Harbor City CA 90710

American Youth Hostels
San Diego Council
1031 India St.
San Diego CA 92101

Sierra Club, Angeles Chapter
2410 W. Beverly Blvd., Suite 2
Los Angeles CA 90057

Sierra Club, Kern-Kaweah Chapter
1000 Pebble Beach Dr.
Bakersfield CA 93309

Sierra Club, Loma Prieta Chapter
2253 Park Blvd.
Palo Alto CA 94301

Sierra Club, Los Padres Chapter
Box 30222
Santa Barbara CA 93105

Sierra Club, Mother Lode Chapter
Box 1335
Sacramento CA 95806

Sierra Club, Redwood Chapter
Box 466
Santa Rosa CA 95402

Sierra Club, San Diego Chapter
1549 El Prado
San Diego CA 92101

Sierra Club, San Francisco Bay Chapter
6014 College Ave.
Oakland CA 94618

Sierra Club, San Gorgonio Chapter
c/o Shipway
1327 Toledo Way
Upland CA 91786

Sierra Club, Santa Lucia Chapter
985 Palm St.
San Luis Obispo CA 93401

Sierra Club, Tehipite Chapter
Box 5396
Fresno CA 93755

Sierra Club, Toiyabe Chapter
Box 8096, University Station
Reno NV 89507

Sierra Club, Ventana Chapter
Box 5667
Carmel CA 93921

California Alpine Club
870 Market St. #562
San Francisco CA 94102

Contra Costa Hills Club
306 40th St.
Oakland CA 94609

Desomount Club
286 Wigmore Dr.
Pasadena CA 91105

Roamer Hiking Club
921 S. Leaf
West Covina CA 91791

Tamalpais Conservation Club
870 Market St., Room 562
San Francisco CA 94102

American Hiking Society
Norcal Chapter
Box 11406
San Francisco CA 94101

Alaska and Hawaii

American Youth Hostels
Alaska Council
Box 4-1461
Anchorage AK 99509

Sierra Club, Alaska Chapter
c/o Shanks
524 North Park #1
Anchorage AK 99508

Sierra Club, Hawaii Chapter
Box 22897
Honolulu HI 96822

National Conservation Organizations

Center for Natural Areas
1525 New Hampshire Ave. N.W.
Washington, D.C. 20036

The Conservation Foundation
1717 Mass. Ave. N.W.
Washington, D.C. 20036

Friends of the Earth
124 Spear St.
San Francisco CA 94105

National Parks and
   Conservation Assoc.
1701 18th St. NW
Washington, D.C. 20009

National Recreational and
   Park Assoc.
1601 N. Kent St.
Arlington VA 22209

National Wildlife Federation,
   Conservation Office
1412 16th St. N.W.
Washington, D.C. 20036

The Nature Conservancy
1800 North Kent St.
Arlington VA 22209

The Sierra Club
530 Bush Street
San Francisco CA 94108

The Wilderness Society
1901 Pennsylvania Ave.
Washington, D.C. 20006

World Wildlife Fund, Inc.
1319 18th St. N.W.
Washington, D.C. 20036

Regional Newsletters

Signpost (for Pacific Northwest) ($10.00/year)
16812 36th Ave. West
Lynnwood WA 98036

California Explorer
45 Woodside Lane
Mill Valley CA 94941

Recommended Reading

This list of recommended reading in How To Do It and First Aid has been borrowed from Thomas Winnett's *Backpacking Basics* (Berkeley: Wilderness Press, 1979) and comments on the books are Mr. Winnett's. We suggest you add *Backpacking Basics* to the top of the How To Do It list.

How To Do It

The New Complete Walker, by Colin Fletcher (New York: A.A. Knopf, 1976), hard cover. This is the best book I know of about walking and backpacking. Unfortunately, it is not for novices: you have to know something about backpacking in order to profit from parts of the book.

Mountaineering: the Freedom of the Hills, edited by Peggy Ferber (Seattle: The Mountaineers, 1974), hard cover. This book is written for climbers, but the chapters on "Approaching the Peaks" contain much valuable advice from a number of people with vast experience.

The Sierra Club Wilderness Handbook, edited by David Brower (New York: Ballantine Books, 1971). Originally published by the Sierra Club in 1951 as *Going Light with Backpack or Burro*, this book distills the knowledge of many major Sierra Club leaders. It is now somewhat dated by improvements in food and equipment, changes in our ideas about mountain ecology, and decreased use of animals.

Backpacking: One Step at a Time, by Harvey Manning (New York: Bantam Books, 1975). Written with grace, humor and feeling by the Northwest's leading conservation editor-writer and hiker, this book distills the experiences of a large number of backpackers who work at the famous Seattle "Co-op," as well as the author's own experiences.

Food for Knapsackers, by Hasse Bunnelle (San Francisco: Sierra Club, rev. 1971). This small handbook covers all you need to know to cook for 5 or 50 people in the wilderness. For me, it's a little on the gourmet side, rather than the simple side.

First Aid

Mountaineering Medicine, by Fred T. Darvill, M.D. (Berkeley: Wilderness Press, Tenth Edition, 1983).

Standard First Aid and Personal Safety (Garden City, New York: Doubleday & Co., 1977), by the American Red Cross, is the standard.

First Aid Guide, by the U.S. Forest Service, is less authoritative but much lighter to carry.

Mountaineering First Aid, by Dick Mitchell (Seattle: The Mountaineers, Second Edition, 1975) focuses on backpacking and mountaineering specifically.

Trail Guide Publishers

Appalachian Mountain Club
Books Division
5 Joy Street
Boston MA 02108

Backcountry Publications
P.O. Box 175
Woodstock VT 05091

Binford and Mort
2536 S.E. Eleventh
Portland OR 97202

Orrin H. Bonney
627 East 14th St.
Houston TX 77008

Contemporary Books
180 No. Michigan Ave.
Chicago IL 60601

Continental Divide Trail Society
P.O. Box 30002
Bethesda MD 20814

DeLorme Publishing Co.
P.O. Box 298
Freeport ME 04032

Eastwoods Press
429 East Blvd.
Charlotte NC 28203

Falcon Press
P.O. Box 731
Helena MT 59624

Keystone Trail Assoc.
P.O. Box 251
Cogan Station PA 17728

La Siesta Press
Box 406
Glendale CA 91209

Mountain Press Publishing
Box 2399
Missoula MT 59806

The Mountaineers
715 Pike St.
Seattle WA 98101

Nodin Press
c/o The Bookmen, Inc.
525 No. Third St.
Minneapolis MN 55401

North Plains Press
P.O. Box 1830
Aberdeen SD 57401

PATC (Potomac Appalachian
  Trail Club)
1718 N St., N.W.
Washington DC 20036

Pruett Publishing
2928 Pearl St.
Boulder CO 80301

Sierra Club Books
530 Bush St.
San Francisco CA 94108

Signpost Publications
8912 192nd SW
Edmonds WA 98020

Stackpole Books
P.O. Box 1831
Harrisburg PA 17105

Tecolote Press
P.O. Box 188
Glenwood NM 88039

Touchstone Press
P.O. Box 81
Beaverton OR 97075

U. of New Mexico Press
Albuquerque NM 87131

Univ. of Washington Press
Seattle WA 98105

Wasatch Publishers
4647 Idlewild Rd.
Salt Lake City UT 84117

Wilderness Press
2440 Bancroft Way
Berkeley CA 94704

NOTES